Only the brave or the foolish dare enter here....

LONDON, NEW YORK, MUNICH,
MELBOURNE, AND DELHI

Editor : Alisha Niehaus
Writers : Alisha Niehaus and Alan Hecker
Senior Designer : Tai Blanche
Managing Art Editor : Michelle Baxter
Publishing Director : Beth Sutinis
Editorial Assistant : John Searcy
Art Director : Dirk Kaufman
Picture Researcher : Chrissy McIntyre
Production Manager : Ivor Parker
DTP Coordinator : Kathy Farias

First Edition, 2007

06 07 08 09 10 10 9 8 7 6 5 4 3 2 1
Published in the United States
by DK Publishing
375 Hudson Street, New York, New York 10014

Published in Great Britain by Dorling
Kindersley Limited.

DK books are available at special discounts
for bulk purchases for sales promotions,
premiums, fund-raising, or educational use.
For details, contact:
DK Publishing Special Markets
375 Hudson Street, New York, NY 10014
SpecialSales@dk.com

A complete catalog record for this title is available
from the Library of Congress

ISBN 978-0-7566-2660-0

Color reproduction by
Colourscan, Singapore
Printed and bound in China by
Hung Hing

Photography credits:
Cover Photo © iStockphoto.com/Kalulu
(lock) and iStockphoto.com/Duncan
Walker (album)
Back Cover Photo © iStockphoto.com/Duncan

Discover more at
www.dk.com

Contents

Your Guide to Time Travel

Ready, Set...Read This First! We know you're eager to start your journey, but there are a few things you should know before you leave—time travel can be confusing! The guide below shows some handy signs and labels that will orient you when you arrive at each stop, so give them a quick review. And be sure to tour our training deck—you'll be spending a lot of time on board ships. Then, gather your wits and your belongings: Your adventure through the pirate past is about to begin!

Helpful Hints for Your Journey

Time and Place. At the top of each page you'll see a time compass and a map of the world. The black pointer on the compass shows *when* you've arrived, while the map shows *where*. Red boxes indicate main stops; green circles are detours.

Detour

Main STOP

Destination Stamps. Triangle stamps give your location and stop number, as well as a short phrase to let you know who you'll meet. Circular stamps offer quick lists of weapons or vessels used in particular places and times.

Signs and Ads. Orange signs show additional places to visit. Classified ads give a bit of local flavor—often by trying to sell you something. Keep a few coins handy in case something strikes your fancy!

> **Detour**
> **India** ▶

> Plunder the
> Pirate Round!

WANTED

Jean Lafitte (c 1780–c 1826)
This Haitian-born pirate was wanted for smuggling slaves, but earned a pardon when he helped stop the British from taking New Orleans in 1812. Lafitte was then hailed as a national hero, but this amnesty didn't last long. He soon stole a ship and sailed to Texas to continue his piratical ways.

Wanted posters and news. Wanted posters give profiles of some of the most notorious pirates of each era, while the *Pirate Times* is a reliable source for important current events.

Pirate Times
London Lockup
Cold, dank, overcrowded, and riddled with disease, Newgate Prison was a fearsome place. Staying here for any length of time was far worse than the daily dangers of being a pirate.

All Eyes on Deck!

It's usually busy, crazy, and crowded, but today we've cleared the deck for your first viewing. This way you'll have time to get your bearings and learn ship terminology—you won't want any pirates to think you're a landlubber!

Block and tackle: used to pull ropes and heavy loads

Bowsprit

Just in Case

You'll notice these sections throughout the book, full of advice and explanations relating to life at sea. They're there to help you with basic nautical skills and knowledge—just in case you need it!

Capstan: used to wind up ropes

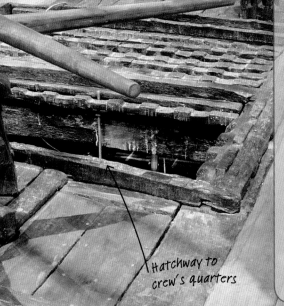

Hatchway to crew's quarters

Get to Know the Pirate Ship

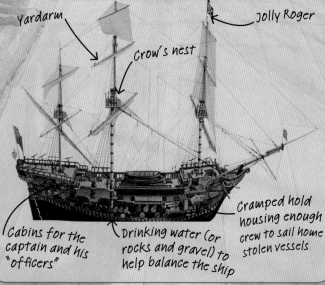

Yardarm

Crow's nest

Jolly Roger

Cabins for the captain and his "officers"

Drinking water (or rocks and gravel) to help balance the ship

Cramped hold housing enough crew to sail home stolen vessels

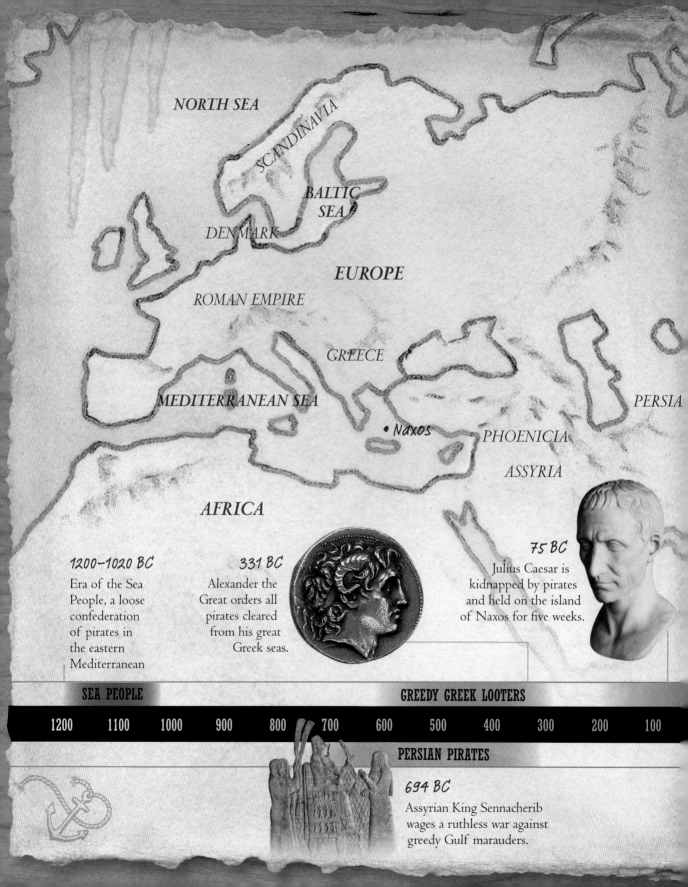

NORTH SEA

SCANDINAVIA

BALTIC SEA

DENMARK

EUROPE

ROMAN EMPIRE

GREECE

MEDITERRANEAN SEA

PERSIA

• Naxos

PHOENICIA

ASSYRIA

AFRICA

1200–1020 BC
Era of the Sea People, a loose confederation of pirates in the eastern Mediterranean

331 BC
Alexander the Great orders all pirates cleared from his great Greek seas.

75 BC
Julius Caesar is kidnapped by pirates and held on the island of Naxos for five weeks.

SEA PEOPLE   GREEDY GREEK LOOTERS

| 1200 | 1100 | 1000 | 900 | 800 | 700 | 600 | 500 | 400 | 300 | 200 | 100 |

PERSIAN PIRATES

694 BC
Assyrian King Sennacherib wages a ruthless war against greedy Gulf marauders.

Ancient Pirates

For more than 2,500 years, sneaky pirates have lurked along popular trading routes, ready to prey on merchant ships. The earliest sea robbers terrorized cargo vessels traveling to and from the rich and successful empires around the Mediterreanean and Persian Gulf—and, farther north, along the English Channel and in the seas of Scandinavia.

1200 AD
Eustace the Monk gives up some of his religious principles to pirate along the English Channel.

ROMAN RAIDERS

VICIOUS VIKINGS

100	200	300		600	700	800	900	1000	1100	1200

STEALING SAXONS

500 AD
Pirate captain Alvida narrowly escapes a royal marriage by fleeing to the seas.

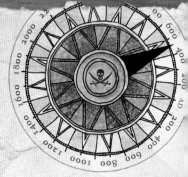

Greece

Greedy Gangster Hideaway.

You're on the deck of a Greek trade ship. It hugs the coast of one of the Aegean Sea's countless islands at a slow, lumbering sail. Suddenly, from its hiding place behind a craggy outcropping, out flies a pirate ship! You're under attack! Scenes such as this are common on these bright blue waters—sailing here is risky business.

Pirate Times

Alexander the Great

He ruled Greece, but when Alexander first came to power, pirates ruled the Aegean. In 331 BC, he ordered them cleared from the seas, making way for Greece to lead the ancient world.

Phoenicians Fight Back!

Loaded with some of the richest cargo on the ancient seas, Phoenician mechant ships were easy targets for Greek pirates. Phoenician war galleys, like the one shown on the coins above, were often sent to protect seaborne targets.

Precious Payload

Silver, copper, tin, and amber, transported by merchant ships, could make sea robbers rich. But while pirates hunted the ships carrying such spoils, war galleys from the nations they robbed hunted them.

Missing: 10,000 drachmae of silver

Last seen on the merchant ship Parthanos, on or about Poseidon 15th.

Heavy Hulk

Slow, heavy, and built to carry as much cargo as possible, sail-powered Greek merchant ships were no match for their swift pirate pursuers.

Pirate Plate

Fast, light, and powered by a crew of oarsmen, pirate ships waited to pounce on their prey among the Aegean's thousands of inlets and islands. This plate shows an attack in action.

Detour Assyria

Sennacherib, Scourge of Pirates

Sea raiders beware! When Chaldean pirates took refuge along the coast of his kingdom in 694 BC, this Assyrian king waged a war that wiped them out.

Assyrian Galley

The Assyrians, who lived in what is now Iraq and Syria, battled pirates in the Mediterreanean in ships like this one. However, no one knows for sure what these frightening vessels actually looked like.

Rome

Seat of Ancient Pirate Power.

Don't be overwhelmed when you arrive at the busy Delos market, but do be careful—you could be whisked away by pirates and sold as a slave! On one day here, as many as 10,000 slaves change hands. And the seas are hardly safer—Roman trade ships are often plundered.

Spain

Gaul

Illyricum

Africa

This is the Roman empire.

Sail in and unload, your cargo is already sold!

The Delos market is the one-stop shop for merchants on the move.

Deals at Delos

In the bustling Aegean port of Delos, both honest and dishonest merchants found buyers for their wares. Here, pirates could sell kidnapped slaves and stolen cargo to wealthy Romans, who would overlook their shady means of acquiring the goods.

WANTED

Roman Renegade
Sextus Pompeius (67-36 BC)

Son of the famous pirate hunter Pompey the Great, this crafty child turned pirate to fight his political rival, Octavian. Sextus raided the coast with great success. In fact, he called himself "Ruler of the Sea"—until he was defeated by Octavian, that is.

Detour Persia

Shapur the Jeweler

In 350 BC this king waged war on sea robbers in the Persian Gulf. Legend has it that he pierced the shoulders of captured pirates, roping them together like beads on a necklace.

Pirate Times

The Great Grain War

In 67 BC, piracy threatened grain imports to Rome. So Pompey the Great took a fleet of ships and rounded up the sea pirates, while the Roman army stormed the pirate lair on Sicily.

Pirates sold emmer, a variety of wheat grown in the ancient world, for a tidy price.

Amphora Few Dollars More

Roman cargo ships provided pirates with bountiful booty. Particularly desirable were the large pottery jars called amphorae, full of valuable wine and olive oil.

Warship Woes

Pompey the Great used warships called trireme to attack pirate craft. Sleek, light vessels powered by three banks of oarsmen and often armed with a sharp ramming prow, these boats were fast and easy to handle. If you check one out, avoid the lowest deck—oarsman there rowed in hot, smelly conditions.

Trireme ★ Trireme
Vessels
Trireme ★ Trireme

Pirates beware: Pompey's on his way!

Just in Case

You're Kidnapped!

Be very careful during your travels in the ancient world. While feasting with a wealthy family, you could be mistaken for their child by pirates expecting a tasty ransom, or you might be captured while touring a vessel. The following tales of kidnappers' fates are sure to terrify potential captors, so make sure to keep them at the front of your mind—just in case you're kidnapped!

Don't Cross Caesar!

In 75 BC, Julius Caesar was kidnapped by pirates. Held on a Greek island until his ransom was paid, Caesar's fiery temper was so riled that he had the pirates crucified alive.

Mythical Mosaic

Bacchus takes revenge against his pirate kidnappers in this ancient mosaic. Swim, pirates, swim!

Bad Luck of the Irish

At the tender age of 16, Irish pirates took St. Patrick from his English village. He felt his eventual escape from slavery was God's doing, and decided to thank the Lord by spending the rest of his life as a missionary in Ireland.

The Kidnapping of Bacchus

My name is Acetes. I am learned in the pilot's art and in the guiding of a ship's course by the stars.

It happened as I was sailing for Delos. I sent the men for fresh water and when they returned they brought a prize, a boy whom they had found asleep. They judged that he was a noble youth, perhaps a king's son, and that they might get a liberal ransom for him. But as I observed him, I felt sure he was more than mortal.

Who's who?

Bacchus is the Roman god of wine and merrymaking. In Greek mythology, he is known as Dionysus.

Then Bacchus, for it was indeed he, shook off his drowsiness, and exclaimed, "What are you doing with me?" The men promised to take him home to the isle of Naxos. I trimmed the sails to carry us there, when some whispered to me that I should sail in the opposite direction, and take the boy to Egypt to sell him for a slave. I was confounded and refused to join their wickedness.

Then the god, pretending that he had just become aware of their treachery, stopped the vessel in the mid-sea. The men, astonished, tried to pull at their oars and spread more sail, but all in vain. Ivy twined round the oars and clung with its heavy clusters of berries to the sails. The sailors were seized with terror or madness. One exclaimed, "What miracle is this?" and as he spoke his mouth widened and scales covered all his body. Another, endeavoring to pull the oar, felt his hands shrink up, and presently had no longer hands but fins; another, trying to raise his arms to a rope, found he had none, and curved his mutilated body to jump into the sea. The whole crew became dolphins and swam about the ship, scattering the spray, and spouting the water from their broad nostrils.

Of twenty men, I alone was left. The god cheered me as I trembled. "Fear not," said he. "Steer toward Naxos." I obeyed, and when we arrived there, I kindled the altars and celebrated the sacred rites of Bacchus.

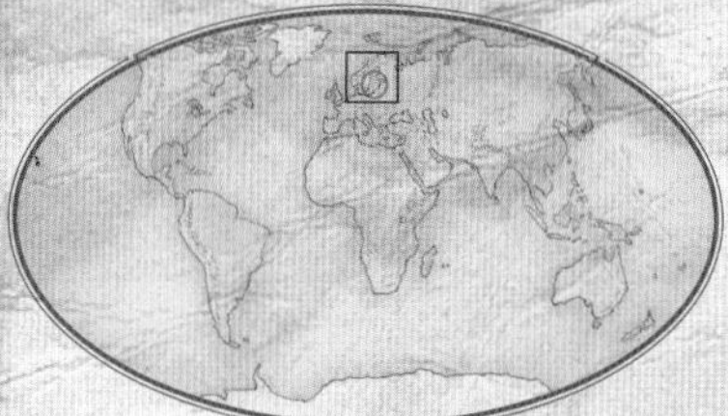

Scandinavia

Home of the Vicious Vikings.

You're enjoying a calm village afternoon, until someone sights a Viking sail just offshore. The longship comes without warning, and suddenly a horde of screaming, bearded, axe-wielding raiders is headed this way! Hungry for glory and adventure—and with a keen eye for the best treasure—these Norsemen attack more savagely than any natural disaster.

Viking Longship

If you're looking for the best of ancient pirate ships, go no further. Fast, shallow-bottomed, and made to take all the open sea could dish out, longships also held up to 50 vicious raiders.

A-Viking We Will Go

Old Scandinavians—people from modern-day Norway, Sweden, Finland, and Denmark—used the word *viking* to mean "going on an overseas raid." On such raids, they attacked abbeys and villages from England to Spain.

Longship ★ Longship
Vessels
Longship ★ Longship

vikings steered with this oar!

Detour Baltic Sea

Stealthy Saxons

The Vikings weren't the first bunch to raid the northern seas. Five hundred years earlier, the Saxons were so piratical that Rome had to fortify much of England to fight them off.

Join the Bearded Norsemen! You've Got the Brawn, We've Got the Boats.

Adventure, wealth, and glory await all who become Vikings!

Hardly in Vane

The Vikings were expert mariners, using the sun and stars as guides. Mounted on a ship's prow, golden weather vanes like this one showed the wind's direction, helping the Norsemen navigate the open sea and plunder new lands.

Glorious Gold

No slouches when it came to judging the value of jewelry and fine cloth, Vikings took the best, then sold it for a good price (or kept it).

Axe
Weapons
Spear   Sword

Axe Questions Later

While they were skilled with swords and spears, Vikings favored axes. In fact, most Vikings could kill a man with one blow of a broadaxe.

Add to this their savage appearance and thirst for glory and it's no wonder these Norsemen were so feared.

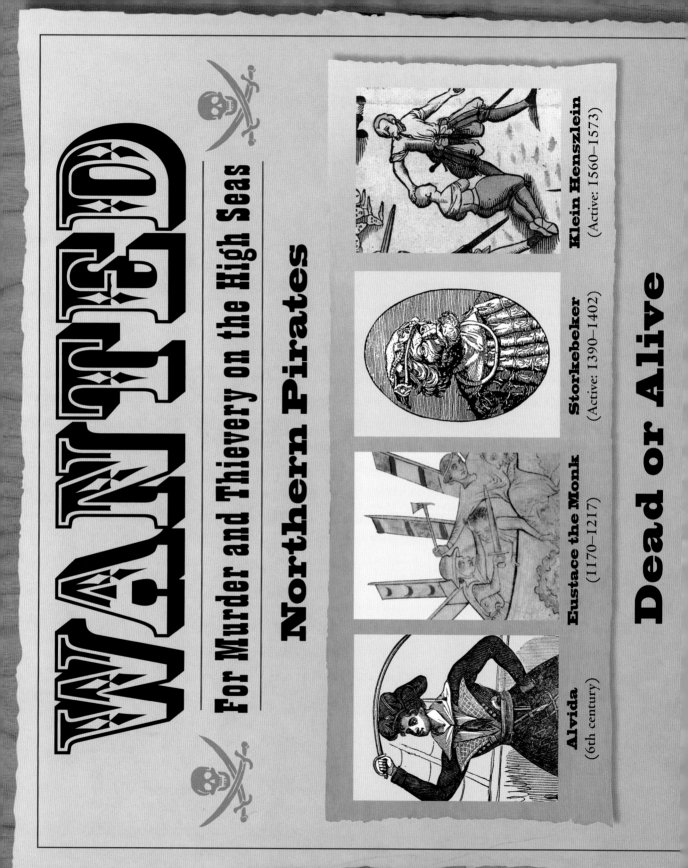

WANTED

For Murder and Thievery on the High Seas

Northern Pirates

Klein Henszlein
(Active: 1560–1573)

Storkebeker
(Active: 1390–1402)

Eustace the Monk
(1170–1217)

Alvida
(6th century)

Dead or Alive

Alvida

The first fierce female pirate captain, Alvida refused marriage to the stuffy Danish prince, Alf. Instead, this stealthy Goth lady set sail with an all-woman crew and terrorized trade in the northern seas.

SCRUMPTIOUS SKULL

Never cross an ancient pirate, or you might end up like this poor man whose skull dangles from a menacing Saxon ship—food for hungry seabirds.

Eustace the Monk

English legend has it that Eustace, a former priest, made a pact with the devil to make his ship invisible. He likely had another run-in with Satan after he went to the French side—and was beheaded at sea by his former countrymen.

Storkebeker

The German pirate Storkebeker took his name—which means "beaker at a gulp"—from the test he forced upon potential crew. They had to drink a huge beaker of beer in a single swallow.

Klein Henszlein

After a career spent menacing the North Sea, the German pirate Klein Henszlein and his crew were beheaded in Hamburg. Their 33 heads were whacked off so quickly that the executioner stood ankle-deep in blood—an effective warning to other Germans considering the pirate life.

Yum!

EUROPE

• St. Malo
CHRISTIAN LANDS

OTTOMAN EMPIRE

• Toulon

SPAIN

MEDITERRANEAN
SEA

• Lepanto

• Algiers

• Malta

• Salé

BARBARY COAST

AFRICA

1094–1300
The Crusades:
battles between
Christians and
Muslims for
control of the
Holy Land

1539
Birth of Dragut
Rais, famous
Barbary corsair

| 800 | 1100 | 1300 | 1320 | 1340 | 1530 | 1550 | 1570 |

BARBARY CORSAIRS

1300s–1700s
1.25 million
Christians are
enslaved by the
Barbary corsairs.

1571
The Maltese
defeat the Barba
corsairs at the
Battle of Lepan

Corsairs

After the fall of the ancient world, groups of seafaring theives in and around the Mediterranean Sea became known as *corsairs*. Hailing from both Christian Europe and the Muslim lands along North Africa's Barbary Coast, they continued to pillage the area's rich shipping routes until the early 19th century.

1627
Barbary pirates found a corsair republic on the Moroccan coast.

11736
Death of Réné Duguay-Trouin, the most celebrated corsair to ever say "Sacre bleu!"

FRENCH CORSAIRS

1610	1630	1650	1670	1690	1710	1730	1750	1770	1790	1810	1830

CORSAIRS OF MALTA

1600–1800S
Europeans enslave between 10 and 12 million Africans.

Stop 4: Mediterranean

4

Barbary Bandits

The Mediterranean

Sea of Slavery.

Almost as soon as it's left the Port of Genoa, the Christian craft you're exploring spies a Barbary galley. Slave-powered oars push the Muslim boat quickly through the water, and suddenly the corsairs have boarded your ship! As they rapidly disable the crew, you straighten your shoulders and try to look calm. With a bit of luck, the pirates will believe you're wealthy—and you'll just be held for ransom. Otherwise, you'll be manning a galley oar for sure.

Christian Lands

Ottoman Empire

This is the Barbary Coast.

Africa

WANTED

Francis Verney (1584-1615)

After a dispute over his inheritance, this Englishman "turned Turk" and became a Barbary corsair. Verney wasn't very successful, however. After raiding only a few English ships, he was captured and forced into slavery. His spirit broken by the harsh life, he died two years later at the age of 31.

Wanted: Strong Christian Oarsmen

No need to apply—just wait around on your slow, vulnerable ships.

Who's Where?

The green areas in this map show Christian lands, while the beige area is the Muslim-controlled Ottoman Empire.

Take a Dive

Both Muslims and Christians made slaves of their captives, and each side could expect terrible treatment at the hands of their new masters. Barbary corsairs prized useful Christian sailors and carpenters, many of whom chose to jump overboard during an attack rather than face a slave's fate.

Brutal Battle

More often than not, attacks by Barbary corsairs were one-sided affairs. Most Christian trade ships were slower than their enemies, relying solely on sails for power. They also lacked soldiers to repel Barbary fighters. Once a sea raider was within striking distance, the trade ship was likely doomed. Land raids weren't uncommon, either—coastal towns in Spain, Italy, and Greece were favorite corsair targets, and more likely places than the open sea to find female slaves.

Pirate Country

Across the Bou Regreg River from Rabat, Salé was a haven for the most dreaded Barbary pirates. In 1627, they took over Rabat and combined the towns to form an official pirate state: the Bou Regreg Corsair Republic.

Barbary corsairs ready to strike!

Detour ➡
Salé, Morocco

Barbary Coast

North African Pirate Base.
Watch out! The Port of Algiers is fast-paced and full of slaves, and you don't want to be mistaken for one. In fact, duck behind anything you can find, because here comes the prince! Locals call him the *dey*, and he's here to speak to his favorite *r'ais* (or captain) about his latest load of human cargo. These slaves are busy scraping and waxing the slim hull of a sea raider, keeping the boat as fast as possible so it's ready to catch more Christians!

WANTED

Dragut Rais
(c. 1539–c. 1565)
A Muslim hero known as "The Drawn Sword of Islam," this fearsome pirate is best known for capturing the Maltese island of Gozo—all 5,000 residents—and selling them into slavery.

Barbarossa Brothers
Aruj and Khair ad Din, nicknamed the Barbarossa ("red beard") Brothers for their matching facial hair, attacked Spanish ships for years. Aruj was killed in 1518, but Khair was so successful that, in 1530, he was given command of Algiers for his efforts.

Gnarly Nimcha
In the 16th century, Arab metalworking was unmatched, so these swords were works of art as well as excellent weapons. Chances are that if you saw a nimcha come out of its scabbard, you didn't have much longer to live, since their beautiful blades made short work of many necks.

Storming Sea Raiders

Filled with slaves and well-trained soldiers—known as janissaries—sea raiders could only spend six or seven weeks at sea before running out of supplies. On these short trips, the *r'ais* was just in charge of navigation. The *agha* was in overall command until the ship returned to port.

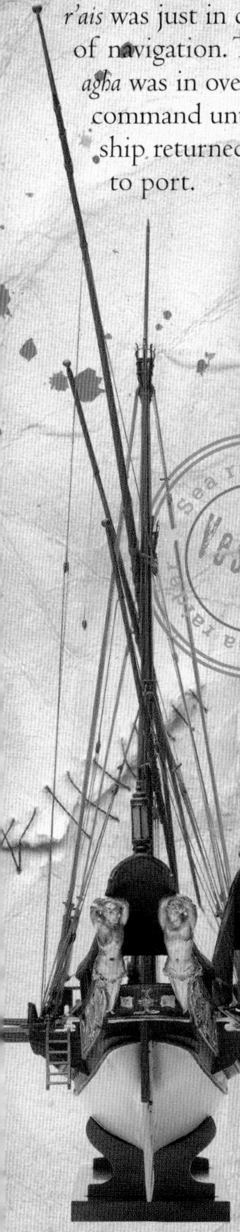

Talking in Toulon

Khair ad Din wasn't just a skilled pirate—he was also an adept negotiator. While working for the Turkish sultan, he helped negotiate a peace agreement between the French and the Spanish at the town of Toulon, as shown in this engraving.

Sea raider
Vessels
Sea raider
Sea raider

Just in Case

You're Enslaved!

"Taken by the Turks"

So many Sicilians are snatched from their beds during midnight corsair raids that this expression—still used in the 21st century—means "caught by surprise."

Fired by religious conviction, Barbary pirates have earned their vicious reputation. Their sea raiders are terrfiying sights for Christian ships in the Mediterranean, and when you're sailing there you should be just as wary. If you're caught by Muslim corsairs, you'll be rowing for the rest of your life—which will likely be quite short. So make sure to enjoy your favorite candy bar and give your dog a hug before you leave—just in case you're enslaved!

Corsairs herd slaves onto a ship.

Slave Parade

As a Christian slave, you can expect harsh treatment from the very beginning of your capture. Corsairs will beat—and sometimes kill—new slaves during the first few hours, to deaden their spirits and squelch all hope of escape. Once back home—where they're celebrated as law-abiding heroes—the corsairs might parade you through the streets to show off their success and newfound wealth.

This end goes in your mouth.

Gag Me with a Cork!

To prevent you from warning Christian ships of impending attack, you'll be gagged with the cork hanging around your neck.

Christian Slaves & African Slaves

Unlike the European slave traders—who stole and sold Africans for money—Muslim corsairs enslaved Christians for religious reasons. Between the 14th and 18th centuries, an estimated 1.25 million Christians were beaten and starved as they rowed galleys and served North African masters. During the later part of this same period, between 10 and 12 million Africans were forced into slavery in the New World. Profit-focused European traders ultimately caught a greater number of slaves than did the corsairs, but because of these Africans' market value, their lives on plantations were often better than those of "worthless" Christian slaves. A captive in North Africa could hope for eventual ransom, however, while New World slaves would never see their homelands again.

"Row faster!"

Freedom at a Price

Clergy and wealthy Christian slaves are ransomed back quickly, often within a few days of capture. So it's a good idea to have friends in high places, who can cough up the money to set you free!

Row, Row, Row the Boat

Corsairs sometimes disguise their galleys as Christian vessels or raise a friendly flag to gain the trust of victim ships. A successful attack means they can replace any slaves who have died at the oars. But after an unsuccessful attempt, Christians are happy to enslave corsairs in kind.

Malta

Mediterranean Pirate Isle. The Maltese galley you're touring is pretty impressive. Powered by more sails—and armed with more guns—than the Muslim sea raiders, boats like this one will finally give an edge to the Christian cause. As the captain preaches the glory of God, you watch the crew closely. What you've heard is true: While these Knights of Malta fight for their faith, they also have an earthly goal—pirate spoils!

Two Hands of Terror

Maltese corsairs fought with swords like this cup-hilt rapier. In their left hands, they carried sharp daggers for closer combat.

The Great Siege of Malta

Strong fortresses saved Malta's corsairs in 1565. When a fleet from the Ottoman Empire attacked, they were outnumbered five to one. The Knights staged a brave defense—even the wounded continued to fight!—and were still swinging swords when aid finally arrived.

Heavy Metal

Heavy breastplates and helmets (called morions) protected the Knights of Malta from their Muslim foes. Still, a direct musket ball to the head meant almost certain death!

Maltese Advantage

Powered by naked Muslim slaves, sleek Christian galleys could make swift attacks. And being boarded wasn't a problem—galleys used their cannons to smash sea raiders from a distance.

Galley Gangsters

In the 1660s, the Knights had nearly 30 galleys. At this time, one-third of Malta's population were pirates, so it's a good thing they had all those boats—and the 1,000 Muslim slaves it took to power them.

Holy Motives

The Knights of the Order of St. John battled Islamic forces for control of Jerusalem. Here, they are loading ships for the Crusades. In 1530, the order relocated and became the Knights of Malta.

Detour Lepanto

Last Stand at Lepanto

The Maltese corsairs fought their last gory sea battle in 1571. They joined a huge Christian fleet against the Muslim navy—and ended the four-hour clash by sinking or capturing all but 40 of the 300 enemy ships.

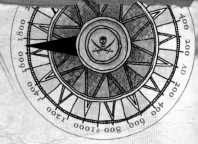

St. Malo

French Corsair Capital. The French call it *La Cité Corsaire*, but the English refer to St. Malo as the "nest of wasps." English ships are often stung, and yours might be, too, if you're on a craft sailing nearby. Training in *la course*, as the trade of the town is known, has passed from father to son ever since the 9th century. So joining the French nest might be the best idea at this stop—and if you're successful, you could end up with a street named after you, as many famous corsairs did. (Send your family to visit when you get back!)

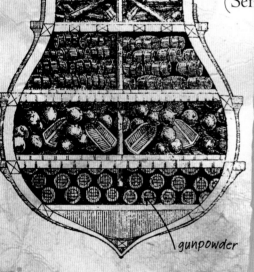

missiles

gunpowder

An Infernal Disaster

The English sent this 85-foot (26 m)-long floating firecracker to St. Malo, hoping to do some serious damage. But the boat bomb hit a rock, and seawater turned the gunpowder to pudding. So instead of devastating the city, the bomb caught only one French casualty—a cat.

WANTED

Jean Bart (1651-1702)

A daring corsair, Jean Bart was the pride of French fighters in the English Channel and the North Sea. Captured by the English in 1689, he escaped by rowing 150 miles (241 km) to France.

Réné Duguay-Trouin (1673-1736)

The most famous French corsair, Réné was in charge of a 40-gun ship by the age of 21. Over 23 years, he captured 16 battleships and 300 merchant vessels.

Bandits or Bankers?

By the 18th century, when this drawing was done, St. Malo's corsair promoters were incredibly rich from the successes of their state-sponsored pirates. Just how rich? So wealthy that even the French king borrowed money from them to pay for wars.

The Kent Falls to the Confiance

Corsair Robert Surcouf (1773–1827) captured this huge 38-gun British East Indiaman using his much smaller ship. After this famous feat, one of the angry captive crewmen sneered that the French fought only for profit, while the English fought for honor. Surcouf raised one eyebrow and replied, "That only proves that each of us fights to acquire something he does not possess."

Barbarous Barbs

Friendly French corsairs sometimes tossed these vicious crowsfeet onto the deck of a victim ship. When sailors—who went barefoot to avoid slipping on wet decks—stepped on them, the sharp barbs inflicted gruesome wounds.

Ouch!

Privateer Pistols

With these flintlock firearms, corsair Robert Surcouf once took on a dozen Prussian soliders—and lived to tell the tale.

Pistols ★ Barbs
Weapons
Barbs ★ Pistols

NORTH
AMERICA

NEW
ENGLAND
— Philadelphia
— Baltimore

London

EURO

ATLANTIC
OCEAN

MEXICO

WEST INDIES

AFRICA

SPANISH MAIN

PACIFIC
OCEAN

SOUTH
AMERICA

Peru —

1492
Columbus lands in
the Caribbean—
but thinks he's
in India.

1540
Birth of Sir
Francis Drake,
England's best-
ever privateer

1243
England's Henry
III issues the first
letter of marque.

EUROPEAN PRIVATEERS

1250	1500	1520	1540	1560	1580	1600	1620	1640

1529
Pizarro ransoms Inca
leader Atahualpa for all
the riches of his kingdom.

1595
English navigator
John Davis invents the
handy backstaff.

Privateers

With so many European nations carting riches home from the New World, the competition was positively brutal. Many governments began to sponsor pirates, making it perfectly legal to attack ships from other countries. These legalized bandits were called *privateers,* and they were responsible for the immigration of many a glorious treasure!

1681
Bartholomew Sharp steals a precious Spanish waggoner.

1775
America's Revolutionary War begins in New England.

| 1680 | 1700 | 1720 | 1740 | 1760 | 1780 | 1800 | 1820 | 1840 | 1860 |

NEW ENGLAND PRIVATEERS

1780
Famous privateer Jean Lafitte is born in Haiti. He'll later pirate the waters of the American South.

Stop 8:
Sneaky Spaniards
5. America

South America

New World of Top-notch Treasure.

You've heard all the stories—gold and riches beyond imagining—and have come here ready to seek out fortune in the New World. But upon arrival, you discover more than gold waiting for you: Danger, disease, and understandably angry Incas and Aztecs could stop your dreams from coming true. You might find plundering a home-bound Spanish treasure galleon a simpler road to riches—and easier on your conscience, since European gold lust will soon spell doom for these ancient civilizations.

Machu Picchu

This beautiful retreat for Incan royalty was built in such a remote mountain location that the Spanish never found it. The smallpox they brought to the New World did, however, and nearly 50 percent of the city died around 1527.

Come Find the Seven Cities of Gold!

Some say they're a myth, but we say we just need to look harder!

Ungodly Conduct

Mistaken for a god by the Mexican Aztecs, Hernán Cortés was greeted with feasts and finery by the king, Montezuma. Despite this, Cortés kidnapped Montezuma and had the Spanish army destroy his great city of Tenochtitlan.

Hardly Treasured

Made of solid gold and incredibly detailed and beautiful, much of the Aztec treasure was crushed or melted by the Spanish to save space on treasure ships.

A magnificent empire was once here.

Inca Invader

In 1529, conquistador Francisco Pizarro led a small band of soldiers into Peru, land of the Incas. He easily captured the Incan king, Atahualpa, and ransomed him for all the riches of his kingdom. When the ransom was paid, Pizarro had Atahualpa killed.

A Golden Opportunity

While looking for a route from Spain to Asia in 1492, Christopher Columbus landed in the Caribbean. Soon, natives showed up wearing gold and bearing gifts. In search of more gold, Columbus claimed the island of Hispaniola and set up the first permanent Spanish settlement in the New World.

The Spanish Main

Golden Lands, Treacherous Waters. As a stowaway

on an English privateer's ship, you're hoping for adventure on the Spanish
Main. And here it comes! Just off the coast of Venezuela, the privateer
spots his prize: a treasure-laden Spanish galleon. Prepare for attack, and
count yourself lucky to see this moment in history! Lone galleons
will soon be rare—the Spanish are about to wise up and start sailing
home in 100-ship antipirate convoys.

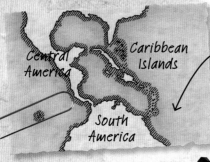

Central America

Caribbean Islands

South America

The "Main" first referred to Spanish holdings in the Americas, but later included the islands of the Caribbean.

Taking Treasure Home

Though most Spanish galleons had
crews of about 200 and as
many as 60 cannons, these big,
slow, and hard-to-maneuver
vessels were easy pickings for
smaller, faster pirate ships.

Cannon · Cannon · Cannon · Cannon
Weapons

Pirate Gold

From New World
gold and silver, the Spanish
minted pieces of eight, which later
became beloved pirate plunder. Each
coin was worth eight Spanish reales,
hence their peculiar name.

Galleon Basher

Privateers made use of the
best technology at hand. Cannons like
this one, able to shoot a 50-pound
(27 kg) ball as much as a mile (1.6
km), made the usual Spanish fighting
tactics—such as boarding and fighting
on a ship's decks—impossible.

Detour
London

eorge the Third by the Grace of

Celebrated Marques-men

First issued by England's King Henry III in 1243, the letter of marque was essentially a license to plunder. Considered pirates by enemy states, these privateers were heroes back home. In fact, some countries issued letters to foreigners—it didn't matter who stole the treasure, as long as it landed in their vaults!

Treasure galleon ★ Treasure
Vessels
galleon ★ Treasure galleon

WANTED

Giovanni da Verrazano
(c. 1485–c. 1525)
Best known for his discovery of New York Bay in 1524—when he navigated the narrows that today bear his name—Verrazano was the first to successfully raid a Spanish treasure galleon. In 1522, he captured three galleons, two full of Mexican treasure and one carrying hides, sugar, and pearls.

WANTED

For Murder and Thievery on the High Seas

Sir Francis Drake (1540–1596)

Sir Francis Drake was an English privateer so feared by the Spanish that they called him El Draque ("The Dragon"). Drake wasn't too fond of Spaniards, either, and vowed revenge after they attacked his ship in 1568. A man of his word, Drake breathed his fiery wrath across the Spanish Main, raiding many great galleons and stealing exotic spices, jewels, and gold for the glory of England.

Thanks to these riches, Sir Francis was a homeland hero. His countrymen also appreciated his brilliant defense of England against the Spanish Armada in 1588. Legend has it that when warning of the impending attack arrived, Drake was lawn bowling. Undaunted, he announced, "There's time to finish my game and still defeat the Spaniards!" In 1596, a tropical disease finally defeated him.

Dead or Alive

A GOLDEN GLORY

Drake was the first Englishman to sail around the entire world, and he did so on the *Golden Hind*. Of course, Sir Francis made sure to gather lots of loot along the way—and to bring extra men to sail home excess treasure on captured ships. (He'd once had to leave behind a big haul of silver due to lack of space!)

THE QUEEN'S BEST FRIENDS

Queen Elizabeth I called Drake, Thomas Cavendish, and John Hawkins the "Sea Dogs," a pet name for the men who made her so very rich. Drake, her favorite, got the special tag, "my pirate."

The KNIGHTING of DRAKE

ROYAL TREATMENT

When Drake arrived home from his round-the-world voyage, the queen's half of his treasure surpassed the rest of the Crown's income for that entire year. She knighted him immediately.

Just in Case

You're Stranded at Sea!

Like much of pirate life, navigating is hard work. You need to know where you are so you can steer toward plunder, but all you have in the privateer era are the tools you see here. So kiss your GPS goodbye and hunker down with these instructions. You'll have to learn to use a compass—just in case you're stranded at sea!

Are We There Yet?

A compass always points north, so you can use it to figure out which way you're sailing. But a compass alone can't determine your exact position: How far you've sailed in that particular direction is anyone's guess!

Sea Artists Wanted

If you're a good navigator, you'll be called a "sea artist," and your skills will be in high demand.

Which of these sea artists' tools do you recognize?

Position shadow vane so shadow falls on horizon vane below

Shadow from shadow vane must fall exactly on horizon vane

Land Ho!

Pirates nicknamed the telescope the "bring 'em near." Clever, eh? Remember, if you can't see land in the 'scope, you can figure its direction and distance by looking at clouds and seabirds.

position sighting vane at estimated latitude

Look through slit in sighting vane

Hold here

The Sun at Your Back

The backstaff is used to measure latitude—your distance north or south of the equator. Instead of staring at the sun to measure its angle above the horizon, turn your back and measure its shadow.

Look carefully... can you tell this is the coast of Panama?

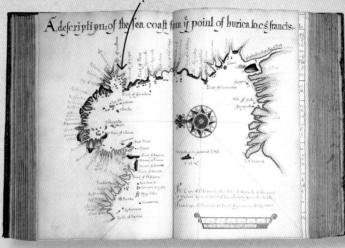

A description of the sea coast from if point of burica to c.s francis.

Top of the Charts

Pirates called a book of sea charts a "waggoner," from the last name of Dutch cartographer Lucas Waghenaer, who published the first such atlas in 1584. Waggoners were so valuable that when Bartholemew Sharp took a Spanish ship in 1681, the crew tried to throw theirs overboard to keep his pirate paws off it. But Sharp caught the book just in time, and it's said the Spanish cried when they saw him take it!

Turn this wheel to the moon's current phase

Tidal Wheel

Tide moves the ship along the sea, so knowing the tide is essential to charting a correct course. A volvelle—or "wheel chart"—will help you calculate the tide from the current phase of the moon. Both tide *and* wind move the ship, so having knowledge of both will get you where you're going faster.

New England

Land of the Free, Home of the Privateer.

Nice one— John Paul Jones has agreed to make you his apprentice-for-a-day! It's too bad all you're doing is scrubbing the deck. Suddenly, Jones cries, "Brits!" He's spied a ship loaded with rice that could feed hungry Continental troops. It might even carry gold dust or ivory. There's no way to know—yet. But one thing is certain: That ship will soon fall into Jones's hands, and you'll be heroes to starving soldiers!

The dispatched Despatch

Philadelphia Story

The largest port in the American colonies, Philadelphia outfitted many a plucky privateer. One such ship was the unarmed *Despatch*, whose crew went on to capture guns from a British ship in the Atlantic!

Busy Baltimore

The first privateers of the Revolutionary War left from this large natural harbor, mostly sailing converted merchant ships. Later in the war, schooners, the ships of choice for American pirates, were built here.

Lafitte strikes again!

Barataria Base

Barataria Bay, near New Orleans, was the headquarters of pirate Jean Lafitte and his brother Pierre. They used it mostly for smuggling and slave trading, but also launched attacks against Spanish ships in the Gulf of Mexico. By 1807, the Lafittes' underworld gang provided about one-tenth of the jobs in New Orleans. Later, this diabolical duo would relocate their operations to the island of Galveston.

WANTED

Jean Lafitte (c. 1780–c. 1826)

This Haitian-born privateer was wanted for smuggling slaves, but earned a pardon when he helped stop the British from taking New Orleans in 1812. Lafitte was then hailed as a national hero, but this status didn't last long: He soon stole a ship and sailed to Texas to continue his piratical ways.

Pirate Times

Stolen Cargo

American privateers stole many luxury goods, but staples were crucial as well. From salt to ivory, they took it all, bringing British trade in the region to a standstill.

Rice

Salt

WANTED

John Paul Jones (1747–1792)

The British called this former slaver (who fled the Caribbean to escape a murder charge) a pirate, but Americans loved him for his daring attacks on imperial ships. During one attack, British guns almost sank him, but Jones insisted, "I have not yet begun to fight!" Three hours later, the British surrendered.

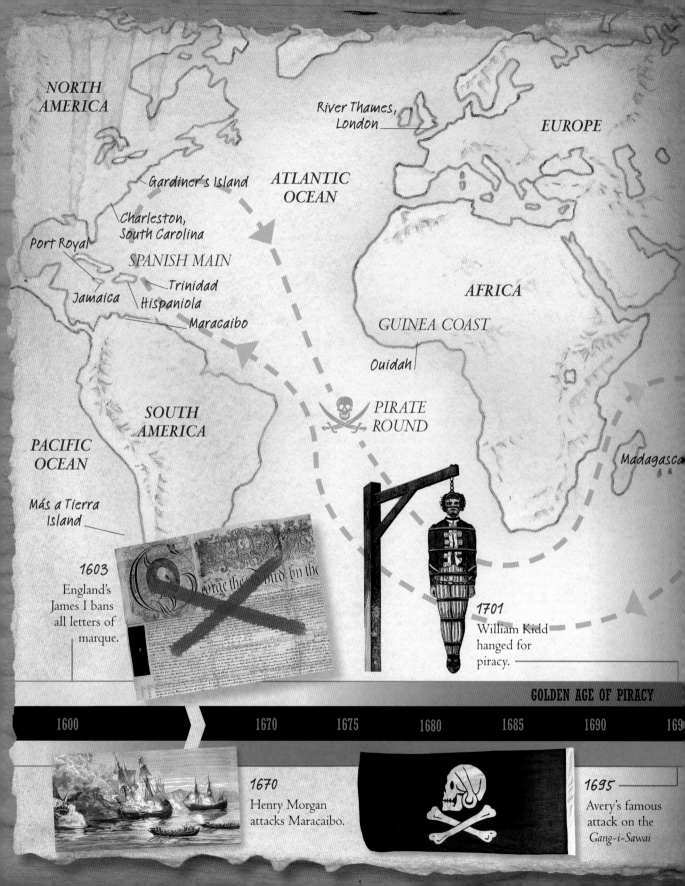

NORTH
AMERICA

River Thames,
London

EUROPE

Gardiner's Island

ATLANTIC
OCEAN

Charleston,
South Carolina

Port Royal

SPANISH MAIN

Jamaica

Trinidad
Hispaniola
Maracaibo

AFRICA

GUINEA COAST

Ouidah

SOUTH
AMERICA

PIRATE
ROUND

PACIFIC
OCEAN

Más a Tierra
Island

Madagascar

1603
England's
James I bans
all letters of
marque.

1701
William Kidd
hanged for
piracy.

GOLDEN AGE OF PIRACY

1600	1670	1675	1680	1685	1690	169

1670
Henry Morgan
attacks Maracaibo.

1695
Avery's famous
attack on the
Gang-i-Sawai

INDIA

INDIAN
OCEAN

Buccaneers and the Golden Age

When the king of England banned letters of marque in 1603, he opened a bloody chapter on the Spanish Main. Lawless buccaneers soon made up for missing privateers, raiding ships with a reckless abandon rarely seen before or since. This so-called Golden Age of Piracy gave rise to many of history's most infamous rogues, along with many of the customs we associate with the word "pirate" today.

1704–1709
Alexander Selkirk is marooned on Más a Tierra Island.

1889
Cruise of the *Alerte*

| 1700 | 1705 | 1710 | 1715 | 1725 | 1730 | 1890 |

1716–1718
Blackbeard's reign of terror

Hispaniola

At the Buccaneer Barbecue. Be on constant watch near this Caribbean island! Thanks to King James I of England—who, in 1603, ended privateering by taking away all letters of marque—buccaneeers now attack and plunder at will. Joined by convicts, outlaws, and escaped slaves, these pirates obey no law but their own, and their terrifying cruelty is becoming legendary. Staying at sea might be safer for once, since many buccaneers aren't seamen, and prefer to attack forts and towns!

Life is Cheap

Buccaneers cared little for human life. They abused their captives terribly, sometimes stretching them on racks until they gave up the location of their valuables. Successful leaders kept their wild men in line only by the harshest discipline—and by inventing creative ways to be even nastier than their underlings.

What's in a Name?

Buccaneers started as pig farmers. The Arawak Indians showed them how to cure meat in smokehouses, called *boucans*. These structures gave the "boucaniers" their name.

This is Tortuga.

Short History of Hispaniola

At first the buccaneers on this abandoned island sold meat and hides to passing ships. But in 1620, when the Spanish attacked Hispaniola and slaughtered their animals, the men got mad and turned pirate. Some fled to tiny Tortuga, which became an important pirate headquarters for decades to come.

Detour
Cuba ⬇

Pirate Articles

I. Every man has a vote in affairs of moment; has equal title to the fresh provisions, or strong liquors at any time seized, and may use them at pleasure, unless a scarcity, makes it necessary, for the good of all, to vote a retrenchment.

II. No person to game at cards or dice for money.

III. The lights and candles to be put out at eight o'clock at night: if any of the crew; after that hour still remain inclined for drinking, they are to do it on the open deck.

IV. To keep their piece, pistols, and cutlass clean and fit for service.

V. No striking one another on board, but every man's quarrels to be ended on shore, at sword and pistol.

Do Unto Others, But Not to Your Brothers

With the buccaneers began the Golden Age of Piracy, when pirates where inhumanely vicious to victims—but pretty nice to each other. Most bands signed a code of fair conduct like Bartholomew Roberts's, above.

Cuban Morgan Crisis

In 1688, famous buccaneer Henry Morgan and 800 of his men attacked the Spanish town of Puerto Príncipe, Cuba. The people surrendered after Morgan threatened to tear women and children to pieces. He then locked them into churches to starve while his buccaneers pillaged all their possessions.

Sword That Took Over The Sea

Legend says the buccaneers invented the cutlass, which started out as a long knife used to butcher meat for the *boucans*. It later became the most common weapon on the sea.

Makes short work of pigs...and people!

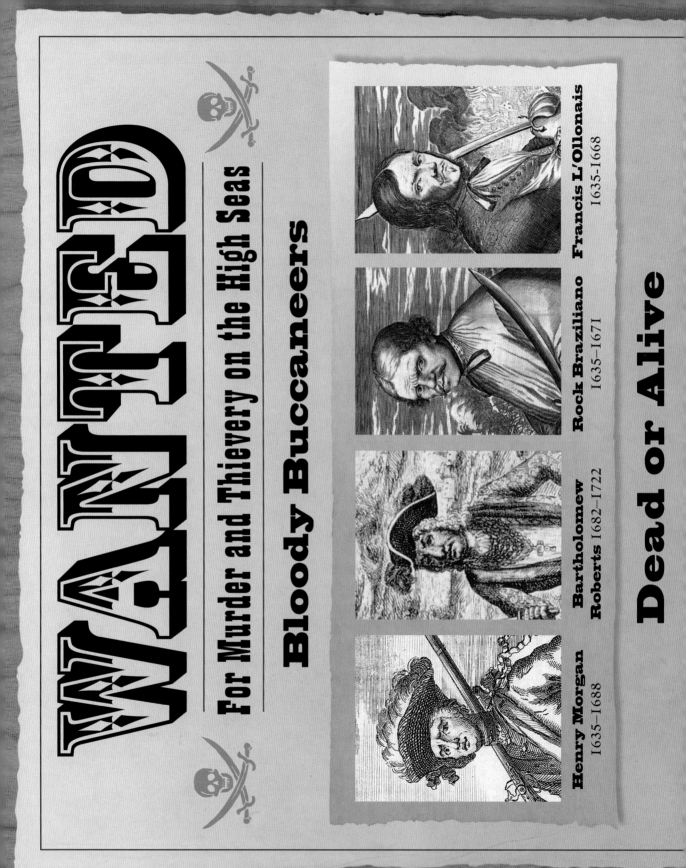

WANTED

For Murder and Thievery on the High Seas

Bloody Buccaneers

Francis L'Ollonais
1635–1668

Rock Braziliano
1635–1671

Bartholomew
Roberts 1682–1722

Henry Morgan
1635–1688

Dead or Alive

Henry Morgan

Smart and nasty, Morgan was known for his daring raids on Spanish ships and towns, which won him knighthood and the governorship of Jamaica. He was also incredibly cruel: Once, he and his men used women, children, and priests as human shields in an attack on Panama.

Bartholomew Roberts

A daring Welshman, Roberts captured more than 400 ships in his four-year career. Perhaps his secret to success was that he never swore, always observed the Sabbath, and drank nothing stronger than tea.

Roberts's Jolly Roger

Rock Braziliano

A Dutchman, Rock got his nickname from a long stint in Brazil. He was so nasty that he had two farmers spit-roasted alive when they wouldn't hand over their delicious pigs. Often drunk, Rock would buy whole barrels of wine and force people on the street to drink with him—at gunpoint!

Francis L'Ollonais

L'Ollonais, a torture expert, enjoyed burning Spaniards alive, slicing off pieces of their flesh, and squeezing rope around their necks until their eyes popped out. Despite his cruelty, he still had a large following, and led 600 pirates in his famous attack on Maracaibo and Gibraltar. Justice stepped in soon after, however, when Francis was eaten by Brazilian cannibals.

A PIECE OF MY HEART

While trying to find his way to a Brazilian town, L'Ollonais was ambushed by the Spanish. After a narrow escape, he demanded that his two Spanish prisoners tell him the way. When they were silent, Francis cut out one of their hearts, took a big bite, and asked again.

INVITING ISLANDS

There were many rich towns and ports in the islands of Caribbean. If ships couldn't be plundered on their way in or out, daring pirates might make land raids, capturing riches and essential ship's supplies such as food and medicine.

Maracaibo

Buccaneer Bonanza. This afternoon you've decided to take a break from your travels at the tropical lakeside home of a wealthy Venezuelan family. Suddenly a panicked servant rushes into the parlor, tugging a braying mule. The *señora* leaps up. As she scrambles to cram her family's most precious valuables in the mule's pack, you understand her terror: Captain Henry Morgan and his buccaneers are on their way, and it's time to get out of town.

This is Maracaibo.

This is Morgan's attack on Maracaibo.

Not-so-lovely Lakeside

Maracaibo, Venezuela, is separated from the Pacific Ocean by a lake. When Morgan's boats got stuck in the low water, the townsfolk had a chance to flee. Many did—but the pirates eventually tracked them down.

Morgan's Monsters

Morgan and his men were a dangerous and dastardly band of brigands. Terrorizing forts and towns from Venezuela to Panama and torturing any living creature in their path, they practically invented the term "bloody buccaneers."

St HEN: MORGAN
Part 2, Chap. 4.

BUCANIERS
OF
AMERICA:
Or, a True
ACCOUNT
OF THE
Most Remarkable Assaults
Committed of late Years upon the Coasts of
The West-Indies,
By the BUCANIERS of Jamaica and Tortuga,
Both ENGLISH and FRENCH.
Wherein are contained more especially,
The unparallel'd Exploits of Sir Henry Morgan, our English
Jamaican Hero, who sack'd Puerto Velo, burnt Panama, &c.
Written originally in Dutch, by John Esquemeling, one of the Bucaniers,
who was present at those Tragedies; and Translated into Spanish by
Alonso de Bonne-maison, M. D. &c.
The Second EDITION, Corrected, and Enlarged with two
Additional Relations, viz. the one of Captain Cook, and the other of
Captain Sharp.
Now faithfully rendred into English.
LONDON: Printed for William Crooke, at the Green Dra-
gon without Temple-bar. 1684.

Going Dutch

Bucaniers author Alexandre Exquemeling arrived in the Caribbean as an indentured servant, but later learned medicine and was freed. He served as Morgan's surgeon until 1672, when he tired of piracy and settled in Holland. Although it eventually appeared in many different languages, his book was originally published in Dutch.

1678 Bestseller

The first—and most influential—book on pirates, *The Bucaniers of America*, is filled with tales of daring raids, terrible torture, and exciting escapes. The stories are so horrific and thrilling that many thought the author had exaggerated some events—or made them up. In fact, Henry Morgan himself sued for libel, and won a settlement of 200 pounds.

Morgan's Attack on Maracaibo, an excerpt from *The Bucaniers of America*:

As soon as they entered the town the Pirates searched every corner thereof, to see if they could find any people that were hidden who might offend them unawares. Not finding anybody, every party, according as they came out of their several ships, chose what houses they pleased to themselves, the best they could find. The church was deputed for the common corps de garde, where they lived after their military manner, committing many insolent actions. The next day after their arrival, they sent a troop of one hundred men to seek for the inhabitants and their goods. These returned the next day following, bringing with them to the number of thirty persons, between men, women and children, and fifty mules laden with several good merchandize. All these miserable prisoners were put to the rack, to make them confess where the rest of the inhabitants were and their goods. Amongst other tortures then used, one was to stretch their limbs with cords, and at the same time beat them with sticks and other instruments. Others had burning matches placed betwixt their fingers, which were thus burnt alive. Others had slender cords or matches twisted about their heads, till their eyes burst out of the skull. Thus all sort of inhuman cruelties were executed upon those innocent people. Those who would not confess, or who had nothing to declare, died under the hands of those tyrannical men. These tortures and racks continued for the space of three whole weeks; in which time they ceased not to send out, daily, parties of men to seek for more people to torment and rob; they never returning home without booty and new riches.

Just in case

You're Attacked!

The Spanish Main is seriously dangerous territory. You never know when a pirate ship will strike, so you'd better get familiar with the language of Jolly Rogers, and practice with the weapons shown here—just in case you're attacked!

Well-made or not, it's scary!

Feeling Crafty?

Any pirate who can use a needle—or paint a rough skull—can make a Jolly Roger. Or this widow on New Providence will be happy to stitch one up in exchange for a bottle of brandy.

Dead Red

Not all pirate flags are black—flying a red flag means that they'll give no mercy. The name "Jolly Roger" may come from the French *jolie rouge*, meaning "pretty red."

No Laughing Matter

Pirates call Death "Old Roger." He's shown here drinking with a pirate, so it's not hard to imagine that the pirate flag may be nicknamed after this jolly guy. Either way, the sight of a Jolly Roger is no laughing matter!

All Hands on Deck!

Prepare for attack! Here come the pirates, making their most terrifying threats. That's likely all they'll need—most crews surrender to pirate intimidation long before the battle. Still, you never know whose ship you'll be on—the crew might be brave enough to fight. So sharpen your cutlass, mate!

Tools of the Trade

Pistol: Packs a Punch. Tuck a light gun into your waistband and you're ready when pirates storm aboard your ship. It only fires one shot, but it also makes a good club!

Axe: It Slices, It Dices… Pirates use axes to help them climb the high, wooden sides of ships. But once they're on deck, you can use an axe to defend yourself!

Cutlass: Not Your Father's Oldsmobile. With its short, broad blade, you can swing the cutlass on deck with little fear of slicing essential ship parts—and certainty that you can cut up any pirate who happens to get in your way.

Dagger: "Say Hello to My Little Friend!" Small, sharp, and great for hiding under your clothes for a sneak attack, you'll be glad to have one or two daggers for fighting below decks, where it's too crowded to swing a sword.

Jamaica

On the Slave Trade Triangle.

You crouch behind the rigging of a pirate ship focused on its prey: a slaver leaving Africa with valuable cargo. The slave trade is incredibly profitable during the 17th and 18th centuries, when slaves sell in the Americas for ten to fifteen times their cost. These pirates want a piece of the booty! Slave ships are such popular targets that pirates and slave traders have become known by a single name— "picaroon," since the two jobs often go hand in hand.

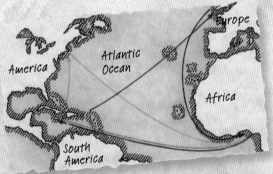

Slave Triangle

Ships from America and England took cheap goods across the Atlantic to trade for African slaves. The slaves then endured a trip back across the ocean, called the "middle passage," where they were exchanged for sugar, molasses, or hardwoods on islands like Jamaica.

Bound for America

The middle passage was a miserable— and often fatal—voyage for many Africans. Packed like human sardines in wretched below-deck conditions, the more than 15 million who survived faced grueling work and appalling treatment once on land.

Surpressed At Sea

Vastly outnumbered by their cargo, a slave ship's crew constantly feared revolt. They savagely repressed any rebellion— which had little chance of success in any case.

A Pirate's Life for Me

Pirate captains in the Caribbean welcomed runaway slaves. In fact, Africans made up nearly a third of some pirate crews.

How Sweet It Isn't!

This painting shows an idealized depiction of slave life on a sugar plantation. In reality, slaves exhausted themselves from sunup to sundown, six days a week. Falling asleep on the job might mean losing a limb in a crushing machine or tumbling into a vat of boiling syrup, but staying awake could mean getting taken during a pirate raid. Then, a slave might be resold— or given the chance to live the more appealing life of a sea rogue.

Cruel Yoke

This heavy iron collar was designed to keep slaves from escaping through the bush. Its long bars and hooks would catch on the undergrowth, snagging the wearer—who would soon endure savage punishment.

Wearing this, there's little chance of escape.

Detour
Ouidah

Take Me to Your Ouidah

When pirate Bart Roberts was abducted by pirates, he took to the life like a fish to water—within weeks, he was elected captain! As the fiendish "Black Bart," he was later responsible for the capture of 11 slave ships at the African port of Ouidah.

Stop 14:

14

Rotten Revelers

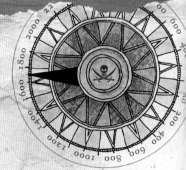

Port Royal

Pirate Party Central. There's nothing quite like a night out in Port Royal. The busy streets are filled with rowdy pirates, card games, women, and bottles of rum. But no matter how noisy the port is, it's still better than the crowded, smelly, leaking ship. So tonight be sure to toss a few dice and make merry, because tomorrow you'll have to make repairs!

Get Two Tankards of Grog for the Price of One! Offer not valid for landlubbers, mutineers, or agents of the Crown.

Gambling Galore

Card playing wasn't allowed on most pirate ships, since it often led to fights. On shore, however, a crooked card game was a common way to redistribute a recent prize.

Pewter Power

Glass was expensive and easily broken, so most taverns used sturdy pewter tankards, strong enough to last through long nights of pirate partying.

A Royal Good Time

The Jamaican city of Port Royal was a magnet for pirates, which was fine with local merchants, since buccaneers were famous for spending with wild abandon. In 1692, the city was destroyed by an earthquake—which some felt was divine judgment!

Rags to Riches...to Rags

Money could buy anything in many ports, and many pirates arrived with more to spend than they'd ever dreamed of. They often squandered as much as two or three thousand pieces of eight in one evening. Two pieces of eight bought a cow, so that much money could have purchased a whole farm!

Careened and Cleaned

To sail as fast as possible, pirates had to scrub barnacles and seaweed from the bottoms of their ships—and remove the hole-boring worms that could eventually sink them. Beaching a ship for such hull-scouring was called *careening* and could take weeks to finish.

Detour ▶ Guinea Coast

Hide and Caulk

Caulking involved stripping the seams between planks, filling them with unraveled rope, and sealing them with hot tar to keep a ship watertight. The Guinea Coast's Old Calabar River was a popular caulking spot, since it was too shallow for most antipirate craft.

Angled blade for hacking old seams →

← Caulking mallet

Carousing at Old Calabar

WANTED

For Murder and Thievery on the High Seas

Calico Jack and the Ladies

Anne Bonny
1697—unknown

Jack Rackham
unknown—1720

Mary Read
1690—1726

Dead or Alive

Jack Rackham, known as "Calico Jack" because he liked colorfully patterned clothes, became a pirate when his navy crew mutinied. A short time later, Rackham took a pardon and settled down on New Providence, in the Bahamas, where he fell in love with Anne Bonny. But Anne was already married—to another pirate! To avoid public punishment, Anne dressed as a man and joined Jack for his return to pirate life. During their few years of successful piracy, Jack and Anne captured a transatlantic ship with Mary Read on board. Having first dressed as a man to claim an inheritance, the "boy" Mary had been serving in the navy, but was happy to hook up with the pirates. Anne soon discovered Mary's true identity and, although the crew knew Bonny was female, the women kept Mary's secret until Jack got suspicious of their close relationship. In 1720, these merry three were ambushed by pirate hunter Captain Jonathan Barnett. Jack and the other men aboard refused to put up a fight, but Anne and Mary fought on until defeat was inescapable. Both pregnant, the girls—Anne was not yet 20 years old at the time of their trial—were only sent to jail, while Rackham was sentenced to death. As Rackham went to the gallows, Anne told him, "Had you fought like a man, you need not have been hanged like a dog!" Mary died in prison; what happened to Anne remains a mystery. There is no record of her execution, nor of her death in prison.

Jack's Jolly Roger

GIRL POWER

Stronger and more courageous than most of the men she sailed with, Mary Read here shows her shocked victim that he's been beaten—by a woman!

CHARLESTON

Anne's hometown was often visited by pirates. At age 16, she met and ran off with her first husband, small-time pirate James Bonny.

Just in Case

You're Becalmed!

Life on a ship isn't all action and adventure. If your ship is becalmed—meaning there's no wind to power the sails—or there aren't any galleons to chase, boredom can be as much trouble as a torrential storm. Still, the downtime can provide a valuable opportunity to take care of some things you put on the back burner during the killing and pillaging. So whether you're repairing the sails or cashing in on a missing limb, the information on these pages should come in handy—just in case you're becalmed!

Here comes trouble!

By Hook or By Peg

When your injured hand or leg gets sawed off, you'll need to put something in its place. Anything on board is fair game—chunks of timber make nice wooden legs, according to François le Clerc, one of the few pirates known to have had one!

Learning the Ropes

Ropes and sails need constant repair. It's always easier to steal them from your victims, but even so, you'll probably spend a lot of time fixing these essential ship's parts.

Fix it or steal someone else's?

Rats!

These furry little fiends find their way onto every ship to gobble up provisions and spread disease. Hungry rats will even gnaw at the wooden hull, making holes that can sink you. If only you could drown them in the nasty bilgewater on the lowest deck!

spoon, to scoop shots from wounds

sharp knife for quick cuts

No Flogs Allowed

Although pirate ships are run democratically, punishment can still be harsh. If you break the rules, you could be keel-hauled (dragged by a rope under the bottom of the ship) or marooned on an island. Chances are you won't be flogged, however, as this practice was often scorned due to its association with the navy.

The Doctor Will See You Now

Careful there, matey! If you get a splinter or take a fall from the rigging, you're out of luck: There's nothing to do for bad injuries except sew the cut shut and hope. Surgery usually leads to an infection which, in turn, likely leads to death. Still, be glad the ship's carpenter—the closest thing you've got to a doctor—carries a helpful kit like the one above.

Pirate Insurance

Under the pirate health care system, anyone who gets badly hurt during a voyage gets a bonus from the ship's coffers. The chart at left shows how much you'll get if you lose something important.

Loss of:	Gold coins:
an eye	100
a finger	100
right arm	600
left arm	500
right leg	500
left leg	400

The Pirate Crew

Captain Chosen for his daring and admired for his cruelty, the captain's power is absolute only in time of action or chase.

Quartermaster As the second-in-command, the quartermaster is in charge of the men when the ship is not in action.

Sailing Master Sailing masters must be well trained in navigation. As a hot commodity, they are prime targets for pirate kidnapping.

Gunner The gunner is in charge of cannons, powder supplies, and heavy armaments.

Boatswain The boatswain (or "bosun") supervises the maintenance of the vessel.

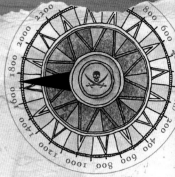

Madagascar

Pirate Paradise. The Spanish Main's treasure is all but gone, so pirates have turned to the next big thing: the rich trading ships in the Indian Ocean. Filled with silk, china, jewels, and spices, they're luring everyone who's anyone to the "pirate round" (the route from the American colonies, around Africa, to India and back). At the center of this route is the island of Madagascar—one of the most notorious pirate headquarters of all time.

Indian Ocean

← Madagascar

Spicy Seas

Spices were in great demand in Europe, but pirates often dumped them overboard, as they were bulky and hard to sell.

Tea

Plunder the Pirate Round!

See the world! Get Rich! Retire early with only minimal dismemberment!

Easy Pickins

From their base in Madagascar, 249 miles (400 km) from the African coast, pirates could launch attacks and retreat to safety in a short time.

Cloves

Outlaw Oasis

Friendly natives and the lack of bothersome European colonists led some pirates to set up small kingdoms on Madagascar. Popular legend says they lived like princes, but they built a fort on an offshore island just in case.

Pirate Times

Biggest Haul Ever!

In 1695, Henry Avery captured the *Gang-i-Sawai*, which was carrying treasure and pilgrims to Mecca. After torturing those aboard to find all the loot, each crewman got the equivalent of three million dollars!

Lush Landscape

More like a small continent than an island, Madagascar today is lush and exotic, much as it was when pirates settled here in the 17th century.

Avery's Jolly Roger

Henry Avery (1665-c. 1728)

Avery's treatment of the *Gang-i-Sawai's* crew and passengers angered India's Mogul ruler, who put a price on the pirate's head. Still, Avery was never caught, and all records end in 1696. He is rumored to have slipped back into England under an alias and died a pauper, without money for a coffin.

WANTED

Charlotte de Berry (c. 1636-unknown)

Although likely invented by a 19th-century author, Charlotte de Berry is still a colorful character. After joining the British navy while disguised as a man, she supposedly took over her ship and led a series of raids along the Guinea Coast of Africa.

WANTED

For Murder and Thievery on the High Seas

Blackbeard (c. 1680–1718)

A lthough his reign of terror only lasted from 1716–1718, Blackbeard is still the most infamous pirate of all time. Born Edward Teach, this vicious villain fought with six pistols slung across his chest and smoking hemp cords twisted into his hair, which made terrifying black smoke swirl around his head. Even his crew was afraid of him—he once reportedly shot a deckhand, saying, "If I don't shoot one every now and again, they'll forget who I am." Indeed, they remembered, as

HACK JOB
In love with a woman who had given a ring to another sailor, Blackbeard attacked his rival's ship, chopped off the man's bejeweled hand, and sent it to their sweetheart in a box. She fainted, and later died of grief.

did the people of Charleston, South Carolina, whose port the pirate blockaded. It took their mayor days to give into Blackbeard's famous demand: a chest of medicine.

Dead or Alive

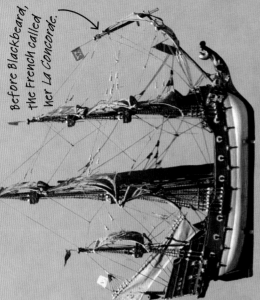

Before Blackbeard, the French called her *La Concorde*.

SWEET REVENGE

A stolen French slaver refitted with 40 cannons, the *Queen Anne's Revenge* was Blackbeard's flagship. Its cannons were often filled with the typical pirate shot: nails, spikes, and bolts meant to rip sails and shred crew—but preserve the ship.

SPY TOWER

Built by the Danish in 1679 on the Caribbean island of St. Thomas, this tower is said to have been Blackbeard's lookout. Since he often plundered in the area, he likely spotted many a victim from here.

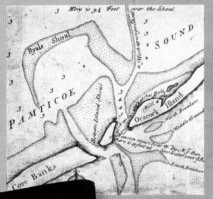

OCRACOKE INLET

This North Carolina island was Blackbeard's favorite resting place. And his final one—after hosting a week-long party for 200 pirates, enraged colonists sent in Lieutenant Maynard.

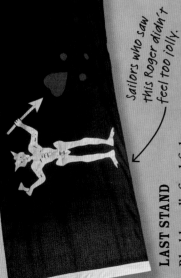

Sailors who saw this Roger didn't feel too jolly.

LAST STAND

Blackbeard's final fight was on the deck of the British navy ship *Pearl*, where he was stabbed 20 times—and shot five!—before he died at last. Victorious Lieutenant Robert Maynard then cut off the pirate's head and hung it from the *Pearl's* bowsprit.

16

Más a Tierra

A Good Place to Get Stuck.

It all happened so quickly: The call of "Reef!" was barely sounded when the ship broke apart. Somehow you've found your way to shore, and even managed to scavenge some supplies from the surf. Although it looks like you'll have some company here on the island of Más a Tierra, most sailors who get stranded aren't so lucky—a slow death by starvation is their unenviable fate.

What a Maroon

Tired of crew infighting, Scottish privateer Alexander Selkirk *asked* to be marooned in 1704. By the time he'd changed his mind, his ship had sailed away. Selkirk spent the next five years on Más a Tierra, 400 miles (644 km) west of Chile.

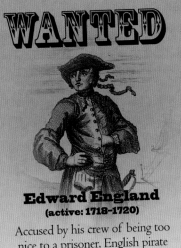

WANTED

Edward England
(active: 1718-1720)

Accused by his crew of being too nice to a prisoner, English pirate Edward England was marooned with two companions on the island of Mauritius. According to one story, they escaped by building a boat and sailing to Madagascar, where England died a short time later.

The Real Robinson Crusoe

Más a Tierra had fresh water and a good food supply, so Selkirk's worst problem was loneliness. In a bout of inspiration, he decided to teach the island's wild cats and goats to dance, and when he was finally rescued, he didn't want to leave! Daniel Defoe read about Selkirk and based *Robinson Crusoe* on the sailor's experience.

powder
horn

water bottle

Pirate Times

Shipwrecked!

Some captured ships weren't seaworthy; sometimes crews got drunk and didn't pay attention to navigation. Either way, pirates might find themselves stuck on a deserted shore.

musket
balls

pistol

gunpowder

Bon Voyage!

If a sailor was marooned on purpose—usually as punishment for stealing from fellow pirates—he was left with four things: a few musket balls, a pistol, gunpowder, and some water. After these ran out, he was on his own. Since there was only enough powder and shot for the pistol to fire a few times, its purpose was sinister: It gave a marooned pirate a way to end his life before his empty stomach did.

Marooned Mariners

Whether shipwrecked or marooned, a stranded sailor's only hope for rescue was to watch the sea for signs of a sail on the horizon.

Just in Case

You're Starving!

Forget what you think you know about food at sea. The roasted meats, exotic fruit, and fine wine are mostly movie additions. The truth is that pirates are often hungry and eat little fresh food of any kind. Some crews have even been forced to eat their leather pouches! Most of what you'll have on board ship was stolen from captured ships. Hopefully memories of your mom's delicious cooking won't drive you crazy— just in case you're starving!

Never Mind Your Manners

Pirates use plates, but that's about as graceful as they get. So forget your manners and chow down pirate-style: Eat with your hands and let food run down your face and into your beard!

Sometimes Cooked, Never Fried

Supplying both meat and eggs, chickens are a staple on most pirate vessels. The sailor's nickname for eggs is "cacklefruit," after the sound hens make when laying.

Tasty weevils!

Dry, crunchy, and extremely gross

Bug-ridden Biscuit

These dense, long-lasting biscuits are the most basic food at sea. Known as hardtack due to their toughness, little black weevils still find them delicious. Like most pirates, you'll want to eat them in the dark, where you can't see the bugs!

Tuna, Without the Can

Fresh fish are plentiful in the waters of the Caribbean. If you're lucky, huge schools of fish will surround the boat, and you can scoop them up like ocean candy. Eat 'em while they're fresh!

I'd Rather Eat My Vegetables

You think you have it bad? Imagine working for Chinese pirate Madame Ching: When low on food, she feeds her hungry pirates caterpillars and rice!

Salmagundi recipe

1 part salted, pickled beef or pork

1 part fresh goat, dog, rat, cat, or seabird

1 part pickled vegetables, eggs, and anchovies

1 part grapes, crabapples, fresh fish, breadfruit "spaghetti," and black banana mush

Add tons of garlic, sugar, honey, salt, vinegar, oil, wine, and cinnamon to taste.

Serve hot from the cauldron. Garnish with musty croutons and wilted greens.

Sea Turtle, Eat Turtle

One of the few sources of fresh meat available to sailors, sea turtles are found all over the Caribbean. The cook likes to keep them in the hold until it's time to feast. Turtle eggs are also a popular pirate delicacy. Yummy!

The Most Important Meal of the Day

On the day that he died, pirate Bartholemew Roberts ate salamagundi for breakfast. A stew made of anything edible that pirates could find, it normally only *tasted* like it would kill you!

Got Scurvy?

Not feeling well? If you have bleeding gums, spots on the skin, or joint pain, you've probably got scurvy. This disease kills more sailors than everything else at sea—including pirate battles!—so the 1753 discovery that eating citrus fruit prevents it is welcome news.

Eat plenty of limes!

River Thames

End of the Line. Here on London's River Thames, you see a chilling sight: a gibbeted pirate swaying in the wind. Your shivers continue as you sail past the pontons, since you can almost smell the crowded holds, where once-glorious privateers now rot in gloom and grime. These days, for pirates facing the gallows or privateers looking at prison, maritime crimes have nasty consequences. You don't have to worry, however—you're just here for a prison tour, and no one knows about your piratical past!

> ### Visit the Famous Execution Dock!
> See pirates get their just deserts over the Thames.

Ponton ★ Ponton
Vessels
Ponton ★ Ponton

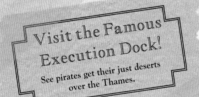

Prison Afloat

First used in 1776, these prison barges were moored in the River Thames. Originally made from navy ships that were no longer safe to sail, pontons were later custom built. Conditions inside were damp and unhealthy, and many pirates felt they'd prefer the noose to spending time in one.

Pirate Times

London Lockup

Cold, dank, overcrowded, and riddled with disease, Newgate Prison was a fearsome place. Staying here for any length of time was far worse than the daily dangers of being a pirate.

Detour
Boston

Gibbet Up

As a warning against committing crimes at sea, dead pirates were often hung from a wooden frame called a gibbet. The corpse was chained inside an iron cage to prevent relatives from taking it down for burial.

How Low Can You Go?

Edward Low (active 1720s) was an awesome swordsman with a cruel appetite—he once cut off a man's lips and fried them, and made another eat his friend's ears with salt and pepper. Still, it's said Low often wept for his orphaned son in Boston.

Laundry hung out to dry

Neck goes here.

Gallow Gatherings

Large crowds came to watch pirate hangings. To the delight of the public, a pirate's last words were often recorded and published.

WANTED

For Murder and Thievery on the High Seas

Captain Kidd (1645-1701)

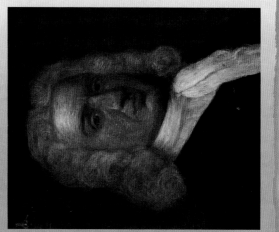

Once a New York businessman, William Kidd was hired by New England's British governor to sail the Indian Ocean and catch pirates like Henry Avery and Thomas Tew. But Kidd wasn't very lucky as a pirate hunter: His first ship was stolen while he was in port and his second ship, the brand-new *Adventure Galley*, sprang leaks. Then, his handpicked crew was forced into British navy service and replaced with criminals, many of them former pirates.

Kidd's biggest haul came from the French *Quedagh Merchant*. But some of the plunder had belonged to the British East India Company, who then declared him a pirate. Kidd tried to regain English trust by ordering his crew to attack Robert Culliford's pirate ship, but his crew joined Culliford instead! With only thirteen loyal men left, Kidd returned to New York—where the angry Brits promptly arrested him.

Dead or Alive

BURIED TREASURE

Kidd buried a huge horde of treasure on New York's Gardiner Island. Some was dug up in 1700 and sent to England as evidence in Kidd's trial. But there might be more!

OBJECTION OVERRULED

Without a lawyer, Kidd was found guilty of piracy, cruelty, and murder. In the early 1900s, papers that could have helped out were found misfiled in a London office.

Captain Kidd

AT THE END OF HIS ROPE

As a convicted pirate, Kidd got what was coming to him: the hangman's noose. The rope snapped on the first try, but the second time did the job. As a warning to other pirates—or pirates-in-training—Kidd's body was put in a gibbet and hung at the mouth of the Thames River. When it began to rot, his body was covered in tar so it could hang longer!

Stop 18:
Treasure Troopers

18

Gardiner Island

Gardiner Island

Burial Ground. It's been a long, hard journey back from the Indian Ocean, and you're finally within sight of home. But Captain Kidd has been acting strange since you anchored, so it doesn't surprise you when he shakes you awake in the middle of the night—you and a few other crewmen are going ashore to bury a chest. It seems kind of a shame, though, since pirate loot generally includes many valuable and useful items that it's good to have around.

Missing: Buried Treasure Map

Last seen at Roger's Tavern. Needed urgently for payment of bar tab.

Lifesaving Loot

Pirates wanted for everyday necessities, and desperate sea rovers would do just about anything for medical supplies. Some were even known to accept medicine as ransom!

Size Doesn't Matter

Whether taken from a ship's cargo or stolen from wealthy passengers, jewels were hard for pirates to divide up fairly. Different kinds of jewels had different values, as did different cuts of the same kind of stone.

Snuff Said

Snuff—finely ground tobacco—became fashionable around 1680. Wealthy passengers often had finely detailed snuffboxes, which were attractive trinkets for plundering pirates.

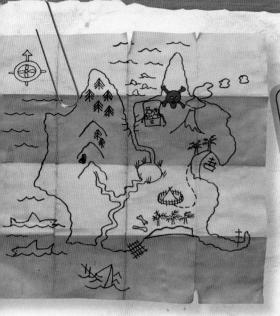

Detour
East Indiaman

East Indiaman
Vessels
East Indiaman

Better Targets

With sterns covered in gold, East Indiamen—big ships that traded between Europe and Asia—were tempting targets. As the gold of the Spanish Main dried up, these ships replaced the galleon as the favorite quarry of pirates.

X Marks the Spot

Most pirates didn't bury treasure. Two famous pirates *did*, however: Captain Kidd and French pirate Olivier "The Buzzard" le Vasseur. Both were caught and hung before they could dig up their booty, but crafty le Vasseur made a treasure map—which he threw into the crowd at his execution.

One for You, Two for Me

Pirates split their loot more or less evenly, but the captain and other "officers" often got more than others. A common scheme was to give the captain two and a half times as much as a seaman, with the ship's doctor getting one and a quarter shares. The carpenter, who did no fighting, got only three quarters of a share.

Trinidad

Treasureless Island.

It seemed so promising when Mr. Knight first made his proposal: *There's untold pirate treasure buried on Trinidad! A dying sailor revealed its location—we just need to dig it up!* But all you've managed to find during your constant shoveling is pebbles and a bunch of mean little crabs, so it looks like you're going to return home with nothing but a nasty sunburn to show for all your work!

Gentle Brains

In 1889, the Englishman E.F. Knight and his crew set out for Trinidad. Knight financed the trip by enlisting "gentlemen volunteers," who paid for the opportunity to come along—and would only make their money back if treasure was found. It wasn't.

Along Came Mr. Knight

In the 1800s, Trinidad wasn't a nice place to visit. With little fresh food or water and shores that were difficult to navigate, the only sailors who went there willingly were trying to avoid monsoons off the coast of Brazil.

Not So Alert

Without a map—or even reliable stories of a treasure—Knight didn't know if he would find anything. He wrote, "I was quite prepared for complete failure." Good thing, too, since the voyage's only real result was Knight's boring book, *The Cruise of the Alerte*.

Pirate Times

Is This the End?

The 1800s are tough times for pirates. No place seems safe from steamships, and man-o'-wars—"pirate busters"—are turning up everywhere. Even the Barbary corsairs have been bombed out of existence! Where's a pirate to go? Seems like soon there won't be anywhere left!

Gold Medalists

Barbary corsairs were finally put down in 1816 by the British and the Dutch, ending hundreds of years of piracy in the region. The dey—or prince—of Algiers released all prisoners that had been captured by Barbary pirates and apologized for the corsairs' actions. This coin celebrates the victory.

Creamed by Steam

The U.S. and British navies built steam-powered ships, which could sail even on a windless day. Often, pirates mistook the steam for fires on board and ignored their pursuers—until the steamships sailed directly into the wind! By then it was too late—the pirates in their measely sail-powered boats were dead meat.

Un-marqued

Thanks to new technology, big maritime powers no longer needed the help of privately owned warships. So, in 1856, many countries signed the Declaration of Paris, banning letters of marque.

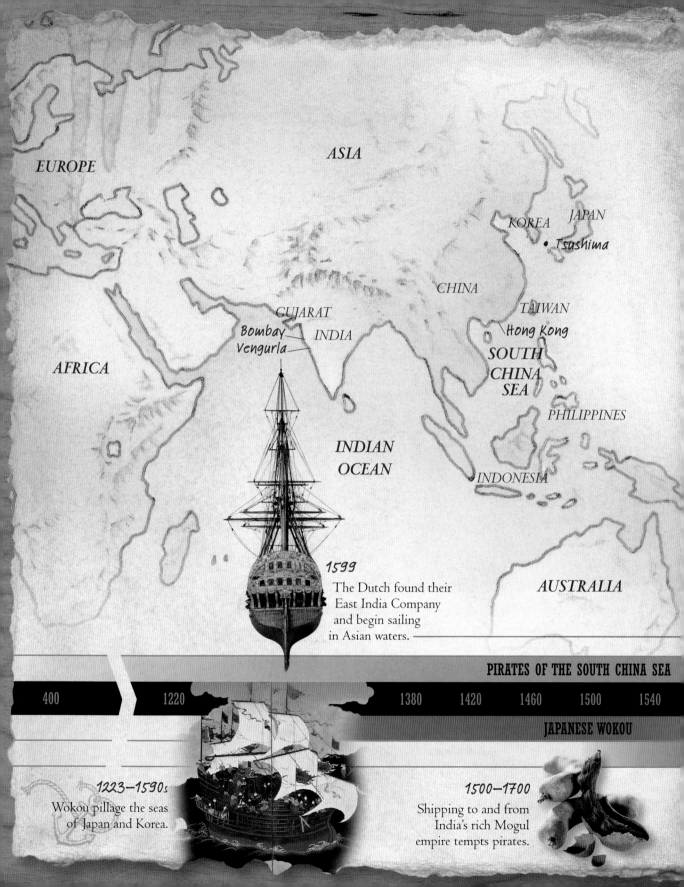

EUROPE

ASIA

KOREA   JAPAN
· Tsushima

CHINA

GUJARAT
Bombay
Vengurla   INDIA

AFRICA

TAIWAN
Hong Kong
SOUTH
CHINA
SEA

PHILIPPINES

INDIAN
OCEAN

INDONESIA

AUSTRALIA

1599
The Dutch found their
East India Company
and begin sailing
in Asian waters.

PIRATES OF THE SOUTH CHINA SEA

| 400 | 1220 | 1380 | 1420 | 1460 | 1500 | 1540 |

JAPANESE WOKOU

1223–1590s
Wokou pillage the seas
of Japan and Korea.

1500–1700
Shipping to and from
India's rich Mogul
empire tempts pirates.

Asian Pirates

The murky mangrove swamps in the seas and channels of China and Southeast Asia were perfect hiding spots for pirate junks—spices, silk, and other valuable goods had long lured traders to the East. This combination made these Asian waters especially dangerous for honest seafarers, as thousands of pirates considered it paradise!

1644
China's Ming Dynasty ends, promising disastrous results for pirate Zheng Zhilong.

early 1800s
The incredible reign of Madame Ching

| 1620 | 1660 | 1700 | 1740 | 1780 | 1820 | 1860 | 1900 | 1940 | 1980 | 2020 |

PIRATES OF INDIA

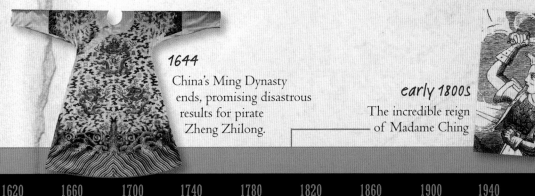

1849
The British Navy destroys Shap-'ng Tsai's enormous pirate squadron.

Stop 20:
Clever Chinese
S. China Sea

20

South China Sea

Navy Smackdown Site. You've never seen a pirate squadron *this* big before. Hundreds of ships, with crews of Chinese, Japanese, Malays, and Filipinos, are awaiting navy prey. On board a pirate junk, you're watching the *toumu* (quartermaster) relay the orders of the *laopan* (captain) when a few navy vessels sail into view. When will they learn that *pirates* rule these waters?

China

South China Sea

Be very careful here!

Borneo

Sumatra

Java

Flying Colors

So many pirate ships pillaged in the South China Sea that they had to group themselves into squadrons, each of which had its own brightly colored flag.

聖 母 天 后

T'ien Hou, Empress of Heaven and Protectress of Ships

Junks for Sail

Junks were converted cargo ships, armed with 10 to 15 cannons. They were so powerful that the navy had no chance—in fact, the Ming Dynasty sometimes offered pirates full pardons and government jobs in exchange for peace.

Bye Bye, Shap-'ng Tsai

This pirate leader owned the waters of Southeast Asia until 1849, when the British navy destroyed his huge fleet. The tide had literally turned against his pirate junks, causing them to fire at each other!

Weapons — Two-handed sword ★ two-handed sword

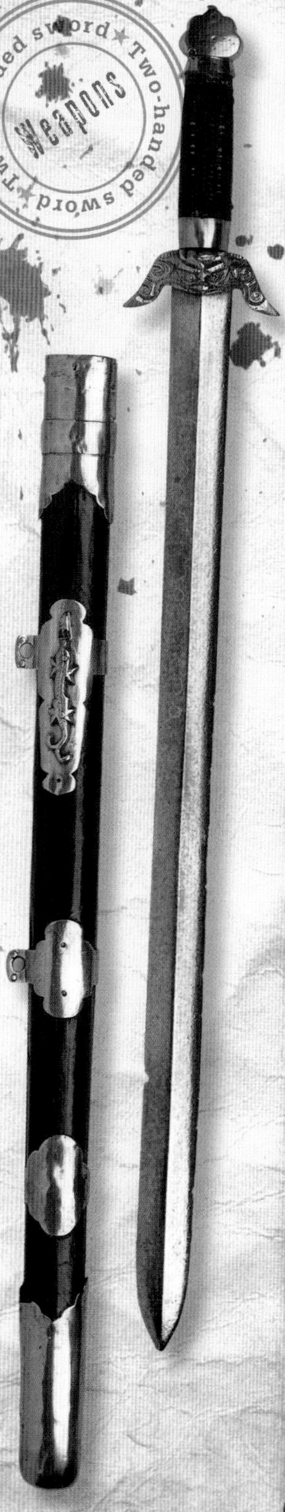

Empires of the East

European pirates were generally happy on a lone ship, or in a small group—and they left their fellow fiends alone. But Chinese pirates attacked each other, forcibly gathering enormous fleets under the rule of one cunning commander.

Ruthless Ransom

Some Chinese pirates would protect their home provinces, but send ransom notes to others threatening to burn houses and enslave villagers if they weren't paid handsomely.

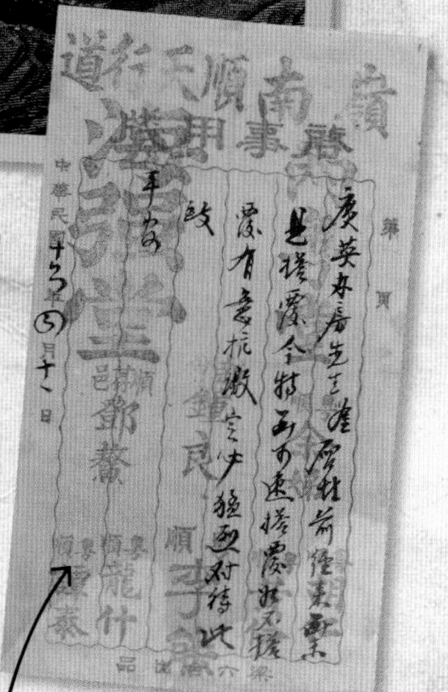

道行天順南寶
漢用事慈
軍廣英夫唐先生准貶將前陸東栗
走掃慶全特五百遠掃慶批元援
震有意杭歡害少強西對信此
鐵言少強西對信此
改
順子六
鄧蕃
顺子
龍什
蒸

The message: "pay me or else!"

Boom!

Lift with Both Hands

Watch out for these monster swords! Chinese pirates liked heavy, two-handed blades since they could easily slice through metal armor—and bone.

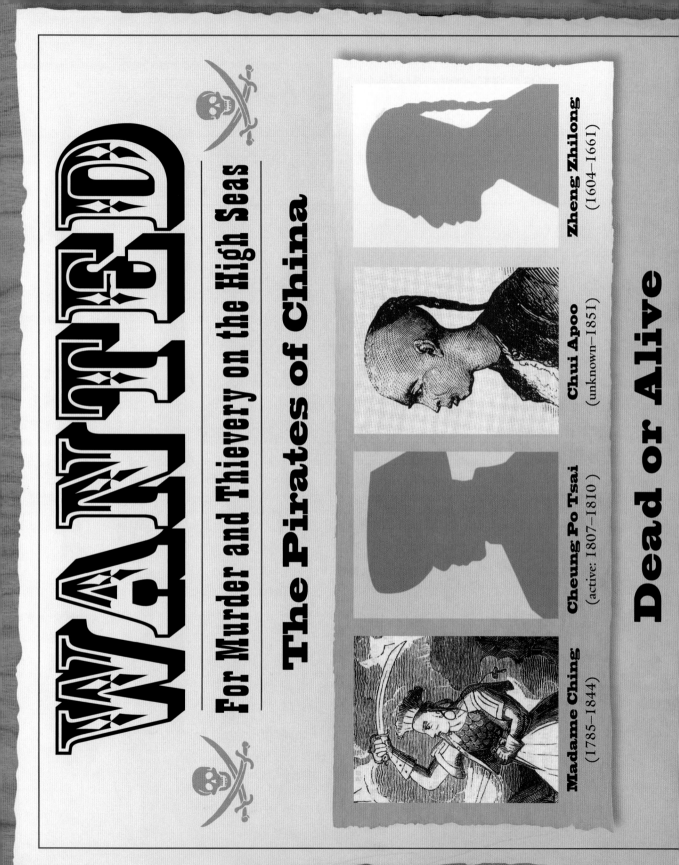

Madame Ching

Perhaps the greatest pirate of all time, Madame Ching commanded 1,800 ships and 70,000 men. She kept them all in order with ruthless discipline—even minor offenses could mean beheading. After years of raiding and outsmarting the Chinese navy, Madame Ching accepted pardon in 1810. She got to keep her fortune, but spent the rest of her life running a gambling house anyway.

Cheung Po Tsai

Kidnapped by Madame Ching and her pirate husband Zheng Yi, Cheung Po Tsai settled into pirate life with ease. Although his kidnappers had adopted him, Tsai married Madame Ching after Yi's death, and helped run the family business until they retired in 1810. His considerable booty is rumored to be in a cave near Hong Kong.

Chui Apoo

Once a barber, Apoo joined the great pirate Shap-'ng Tsai and quickly moved up the ranks to command 600 junks. His fleet operated around Hong Kong, and was chased and sunk by the British navy in 1849. Apoo escaped and reappeared on the pirate scene a year later—only to be defeated once more.

Zheng Zhilong

Sometimes considered the Robin Hood of China, handsome Zhilong stole from his government and European traders to give to the poor (and himself). Officials couldn't stop this incredible pirate, so they offered him a cushy job to join their side. He accepted, built a big palace—and then helped his son, Koxinga, continue his pirate legacy.

NOT A VACATION DESTINATION!

Territory was sacred to these pirates, and they were aggressive about protecting their pieces of the sea. They generally fired upon any unknown vessel that made the mistake of sailing in —even passenger vessels like this 1923 European ship.

Stop 21:

Japan

21 Japan Wave Warriors

Land of the Raiding Sons.
With all the Chinese, Koreans, and Portuguese on the ship, it's hard to believe these pirates are known as "Japanese bandits." Not to mention that the *wokou* have put you in the care of a Christian missionary they took in a coastal raid. Seems these wave warriors will take anyone along for the ride!

Take Two!

Japanese pirates preferred to fight with two short, light swords. They could attack—and defend—better with a small sword in each hand than with one large blade.

Short swords **Weapons** *Short swords*

We Will Wokou

These pirate gangs—known as *wokou*, or "Japanese bandits" in Chinese—raided Korean and Chinese seas and coastal towns from the 13th to the 16th century. During the height of their power, they even pillaged inland down the Yangtze River! Their first base was the island of Tsushima, off Japan's northwest coast.

Amply Armed

Mixing new technology with traditional ways, many Japanese pirates used guns and swords at the same time to bring their devious plans to a faster finale.

Detour ➡ India

Cough It Up

Pirates worked the west coast of India for hundreds of years. One dangerous group was known as the Gujarati Rovers. When the rovers thought their captives had swallowed valuable jewels instead of handing them over, they mixed up a disgusting cocktail of tamarind paste and seawater. After one sickening sip, any "lost" treasure was usually found.

Tamarind also makes yummy curry!

WANTED

Kanhoji Angre (unknown-1729)

An national hero in India, this North African Muslim raided European ships from Bombay to Vengurla for a whopping 25 years. After his death, his sons took over the family business and menaced ships until 1746.

Watch Your Head

The islands of Indonesia and the Philippines have long provided a safe haven for pirates and other inhospitable sorts. In fact, the inlets of Borneo and Sumatra once sheltered fierce tribes of head-hunters. If you decide to pass this way, they'll be happy to invite you for dinner!

Detour ⬇ Indonesia

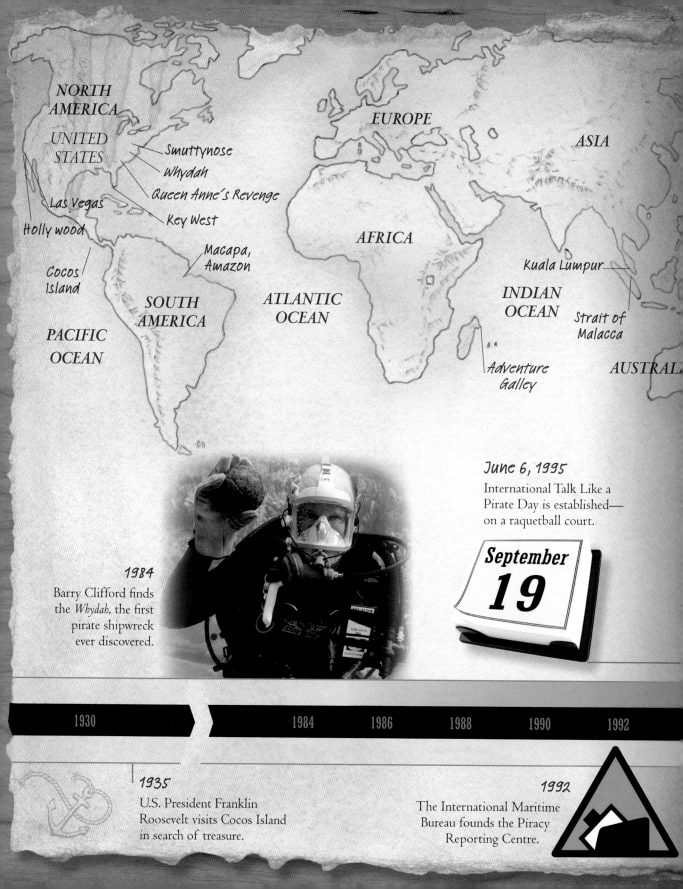

NORTH
AMERICA

UNITED
STATES

— Smuttynose

— Whydah

— Queen Anne's Revenge

Las Vegas

— Key West

Holly wood

Cocos
Island

Macapa,
Amazon

SOUTH
AMERICA

ATLANTIC
OCEAN

PACIFIC
OCEAN

EUROPE

ASIA

AFRICA

Kuala Lumpur

INDIAN
OCEAN

Strait of
Malacca

Adventure
Galley

AUSTRAL

June 6, 1995
International Talk Like a
Pirate Day is established—
on a raquetball court.

September
19

1984
Barry Clifford finds
the *Whydah*, the first
pirate shipwreck
ever discovered.

1930

1984 1986 1988 1990 1992

1935
U.S. President Franklin
Roosevelt visits Cocos Island
in search of treasure.

1992
The International Maritime
Bureau founds the Piracy
Reporting Centre.

Modern-Day Pirates

The world of Blackbeard is far behind us, but that hasn't stopped pirates from threatening the seas. In fact, the same technology that makes modern maritime life much easier has also given today's rogues nifty tools to put to nefarious use. Off the ocean, pirates are popular, too—we still search for their treasure in movies, festivals, and even in books like this!

2003
Pirates of the Caribbean: Curse of the Black Pearl premieres in theaters around the world.

2005
Seabourn Spirit uses an LRAD in defense against pirates.

MODERN MARAUDERS

| 1996 | 1998 | 2000 | 2002 | 2004 | 2006 | 2008 | 2010 |

1996
Discovery of the *Queen Anne's Revenge*

2000
The first Pirates in Paradise festival is held in Key West, Florida.

Stop 23:
Malacca

22
Current Criminal

Strait of Malacca

Dangerous Territory. The captain's call cuts through your sleep: "All hands on deck! Pirates attempting to board!" Even though your ship is fitted with a 9,000-volt deterrent system—basically an electric fence attached to the hull—some pirates might still sneak aboard. Really, you should have seen this coming: This narrow channel connecting the Pacific and Indian Oceans is one of the biggest pirate hot spots in the world.

Machete ★ GPS ★
GPS
Weapons
Machete ★

Missing: One
Boatload of Cargo
Last seen leaving New York
harbor amid sounds of laughter.

Phantom of the Ocean

Some pirates take over a vessel to create a "phantom ship." They repaint it, rename it, and offer to carry cargo. The scheming pirates then sail to a different port and sell the goods themselves.

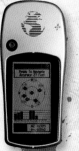

High Tech Heists

Some of today's pirates use the most modern technology, from global positioning systems (GPS) to radar and radio. They stealthily track their targets and often pounce while the ship's crew sleeps!

Don't let this spooky ship carry your cargo!

Old School

Not all modern pirates are high tech. Some—like many who work rivers—are so poor that they still use weapons like machetes!

Detour ⬇ The Amazon

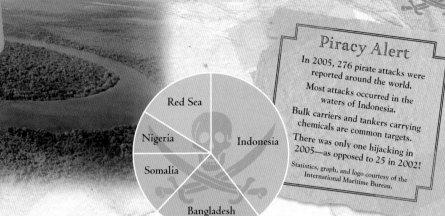

Piracy Alert

In 2005, 276 pirate attacks were reported around the world.

Most attacks occurred in the waters of Indonesia.

Bulk carriers and tankers carrying chemicals are common targets.

There was only one hijacking in 2005—as opposed to 25 in 2002!

Statistics, graph, and logo courtesy of the International Maritime Bureau.

Pie chart labels: Red Sea, Nigeria, Somalia, Indonesia, Bangladesh

Dirty Rats!

In 2001, famous yachtsman Sir Peter Blake was killed when Amazon River pirates raided his boat. While trying to defend the crew, Blake suffered two fatal gunshot wounds. The pirates—who called themselves the River Rats—got away with a spare motor and some wristwatches.

2006 Pirate Activity

Between January and March, a total of 61 pirate attacks were reported. This graph shows where they occurred.

IMB Piracy Reporting Centre

Started in Kuala Lumpur, Malaysia, in 1992, the Piracy Reporting Centre coordinates the international antipiracy effort. Its services, provided free of charge to any vessel, include a 24-hour help line and assistance for shipowners and crew members who are attacked.

Long Range Acoustic Device

In November 2005, the cruise liner *Seabourn Spirit* used an LRAD to fend off pirates. This U.S. military device repels attackers by emitting painfully high-pitched sound waves.

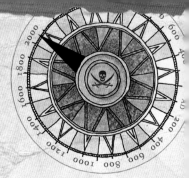

Stops 23–26: Shipwrecks

23-26
Hidden Hulks

Shipwrecks

Big Payoffs—If You Can Find Them.

You won't be the first to search for treasures left behind by some of the most famous—and infamous—pirates. But since you're almost home, why not take a little while to explore? Your family may be waiting to see you, but think how impressed they'll be if you return with a shiny pirate souvenir!

There are supposed to be three huge hoards here—but where?

Coo-coo for Cocos Island

This Costa Rican island is said to be the home of *three* fabulous treasures: a 17th-century haul, the booty of pirate Benito Bonito, and the legendary Treasure of Lima. Hundreds of people have come looking for them, including U.S. President Franklin Roosevelt! Nevertheless, no treasure has ever been found. Even German adventurer August Gissler, who spent 17 years here, left with just a few pieces of eight.

Whydah Heck It Sink?

Flagship of pirate Sam Bellamy, the *Whydah* is the only verified pirate shipwreck. It took treasure hunter Barry Clifford 15 years to find it, but more than 100,000 items have been found so far—including gold and silver doubloons.

Telescope

Bottle

The Real Thing?

Blackbeard ran his flagship aground off North Carolina in 1717. What *might* be the *Queen Anne's Revenge*—no definite identifying relics have been found—was located in 1996, and has since yielded some interesting artifacts, including these items—and a small bit of gold dust!

Bell

A ship's bell usually has its name engraved here, but this one is blank!

Barry Clifford

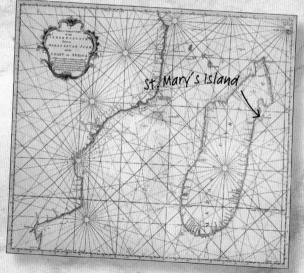

Accidental Discovery

All that's been found of Blackbeard's famous treasure is some cotton, sugar, and cocoa. But what about the rest? One legend says that he buried it on Smuttynose, an island off New Hampshire. In 1820, a man building a wall on the island dug up four bars of silver. Some think this may have been a taste of the pirate's treasure, and the rest is waiting to be found.

St. Mary's Island

Looking for Adventure

When William Kidd heard he was wanted for piracy, he sunk his ship, *The Adventure Galley*, in the bay of St. Mary's Island, near Madagascar. For years after, the sunken wreck could be seen in the water. But time and tide have hidden the ship's remains, and now the hunt is on to find it—and see what was left behind!

Just in Case

You Have to Talk Like a Pirate!

September 19

These days, it seems like everyone's talking *about* pirates, but how many people can actually talk *like* one? After your incredible journey through pirate history, you should be able to impress any landlubber with your corsair curses and Jolly Roger jargon. But if you ever need help or clarification, check out this convenient glossary—just in case you have to talk like a pirate!

Dread Letter Day

The pirate glossary will be really handy on September 19th, International Talk Like a Pirate Day. Then no matter where you are, you can say a hearty "Arrrrr!"

Piratical Fun For Everyone

Clap on yer scratchy peg leg and gather yer hearties—it's time for Pirates in Paradise! Held annually in the old-time pirate haven of Key West, Florida, this festival has songs, sailing, salamagundi, and a super-cool reenactment of the "Pyrate Tryal of Anne Bonny and Mary Read," straight from the real trial transcript.

GREETINGS FROM **KEY WEST** FLA.

SOUTHERNMOST CITY IN THE UNITED STATES

Key Relics

For a look at some real pirate stuff—like a musket that belonged to Blackbeard and a treasure chest used by Thomas Tew—sail on down and say "ahoy!" to Key West's Pirate Soul Museum.

Pirate Glossary

Ahoy! "Hello!"

Arrr! A piratical grunt that can mean just about anything, from "I agree" to "boo!" to "hmmm" to, well, "arrr!"

Avast ye landlubbers! Avast means "stop" or "stay," and lubber is a klutz—so a landlubber is someone who's as clumsy on board ship as a person's who's never been to sea.

Pirate with a clapped-on leg

Aye! "Yes, I agree!"

Aye-Aye! "Right away!"

Clap On To clap on is to add a temporary feature. For example, clapping on a sail means rigging an extra one that you will later take down.

Davey Jones's Locker Davey Jones is a sailor's name for the evil spirit of the deep, as well as a term for death. His locker is where unlucky ships—or people—go to rest their eternal souls.

Dead Man's Chest An island in the Bahamas where Blackbeard abandoned 15 of his own men; the subject of a sea shanty in R.L. Stevenson's *Treasure Island*

Freebooter This term for pirate is from the Dutch *vrijbuiter*, meaning "free plunder."

Go on the account Buccaneers used this phrase to discuss their seafaring life. It was more acceptable to say they were "going on the account" than to say they were off to be pirates.

Kissing the gunner's daughter

Grog A very popular rum-and-water drink named for Admiral Edward Vernon, who got the nickname "Old Grog" from a grogham coat he wore

Kiss the gunner's daughter To be flogged aboard ship

Me hearty A friend or shipmate

Sea legs Sailors get "sea legs" when they've been at sea so long that they never get seasick.

Shivered timbers

Sea rover A pirate or a pirate ship

Scuppers Holes pierced in the upper deck to give surplus water a place to drain

Shiver me timbers A "shiver" is a splinter. "Timbers" are the wood of the ship. If a ship suddenly hit something, its timbers were shivered! Pirates used this as a term of surprise or shock.

Strike the colors To haul down a ship's flag as a signal of surrender

Tip the black spot To make a death threat by giving someone a piece of paper marked with a black smudge.

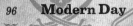

Stop 29

Hollywood

27

★ Heroic Heartthrobs ★

Hollywood

Where Swashbucklers Meet the Silver Screen.

You've seen probably seen plenty of pirate movies. After all, Hollywood's been making them since 1905's silent saga *The River Pirates*. But now you can watch pirate movies with a critical eye—since you've been there, you know what's true and what's exaggerated. Notice how the screen has turned some nasty pirate villains into swashbuckling heroes?

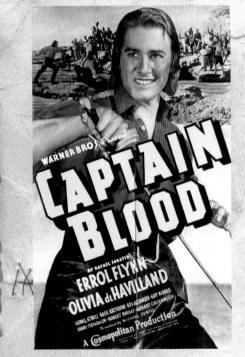

Pirate's Honor

In 1987's *The Princess Bride*, Westley is kidnapped by pirates, only to become their leader—the Dread Pirate Roberts. He learns sword fighting and outsmarts all his opponents, but is still an honorable man—unlike many other pirates, real or fictional. Plus, he gets the girl!

Original Swashbuckler

Hollywood made a fortune on *Captain Blood*, which made an overnight star of Errol Flynn. Many of the themes in pirate movies today—like the pirate as a hero—first appeared in this 1935 film.

1995's Rare Pirate Bomb

Not all pirate movies are hits. The action-packed film *Cutthroat Island*, about a female pirate (a plot that Hollywood hasn't tried before or since) cost $100 million to make but only made $10 million in theaters.

Pirate Times

Pirates of the Caribbean I, II, & III

The most popular pirate movies of all time, these 2003, 2006, and 2007 blockbusters cram tons of pirate lore into comic action-adventure classics!

Geena Davis makes one awesome pirate!

Detour
Las Vegas

Don't Bet On It

Profiting from piratemania isn't just for Hollywood. Las Vegas got in on the deal in 1993, when the Treasure Island hotel opened on the famous Strip. The 2,885-room hotel once featured ship-to-ship pirate battles twice a day, but has since tried to sever ties with its pirate past.

Detour
Neverland

Hooked

Captain Hook blends all of the most fearsome bits of pirate legend into one character. Still, he's found his villainous way into many hearts, as evidenced by the popularity of the 1991 film *Hook*, starring Dustin Hoffman as the captain himself.

The Adventure In Review

Your Complete Pirate Timelime. From Pompey's Rome to Avery's Madagascar, you've journeyed through lots of grisly epochs. To help keep it all straight, this timeline shows the major eras of maritime mayhem, along with each age's most vicious vessel. Looking back, it's a miracle you came out in one piece!

Roman Trireme

For making short work of pirate ships, the ramming prow on this boat was sure impressive!

Greek Merchant Ship

Remember how you bravely defended one of these slow boats from pirate attack?

1200	1000	800	600	400	200	0	200	400

SEA PEOPLE   GREEDY GREEK LOOTERS   ROMAN RAIDERS

PERSIAN PIRATES   STEALING SAXONS

Viking Vessel

You thought these Norsemen were the scariest pirates on the seas. Until you met the buccaneers, that is!

Chinese Junk

They don't look that dangerous, but you learned just how nasty these ships could be, especially to the poor navy.

Columbus's Voyage

Getting lost was never so profitable, before 1492 or since!

Christian Galley

Treatment of slaves on these craft brought tears to your eyes.

East Indiaman

Watching pirates pounce on these beauties was awesome, right?

Spanish Galleon

Do something nice for your family and friends with the treasure you took from this ship!

Modern Freighter

Good of you to have let those Swedes know the boat they almost hired was a phantom.

Drake's Golden Hind

How strange you never ran into this ship—it sailed all the way around the world, after all.

600   800   1000   1200   1400   1600   1800   2000   2200

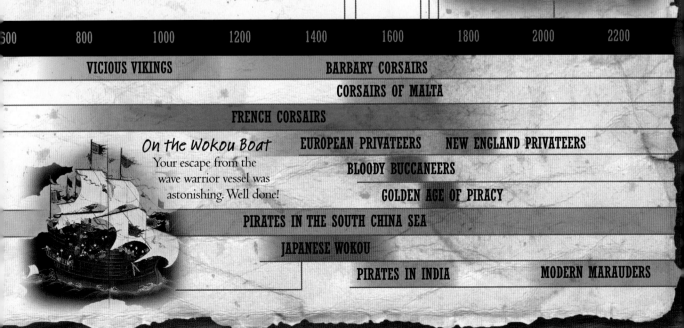

VICIOUS VIKINGS

BARBARY CORSAIRS

CORSAIRS OF MALTA

FRENCH CORSAIRS

On the Wokou Boat

Your escape from the wave warrior vessel was astonishing. Well done!

EUROPEAN PRIVATEERS   **NEW ENGLAND PRIVATEERS**

BLOODY BUCCANEERS

GOLDEN AGE OF PIRACY

PIRATES IN THE SOUTH CHINA SEA

JAPANESE WOKOU

PIRATES IN INDIA   **MODERN MARAUDERS**

*W*elcome back. We hope your voyage through pirate time didn't tire you out—there's more excitement in store!

Facts are only one part of the pirate world. Authors' fantastic imaginations and deft storytelling make up the others—those we most remember: the romance and thrills of heroes interacting with sea rogues on the page. In fact, fictional stories are so influential that much of their lore has blended with reality. Talking parrots as pirate pets? That's from *Treasure Island*. Walking the plank as a popular punishment? Charles Ellms thought it up! Still, no matter what their origin, these legends keep us dreaming of lives we've never known, and of possibilities for our own. Maybe they'll even inspire you to pen a pirate adventure yourself!

There are so many pirate books that we could never include them all here! In fact, we've only been able to give a taste of the most famous stories. So if you want to read these adventures all the way through— and we hope you do!—visit your local bookstore or library. (And be sure to take our list of the most excellent pirate titles with you—print it out from http://www.kiddk.com/piratepedia!)

Classic Pirate Literature

Treasure Island

Treasure Island is perhaps the most popular pirate story of all time. When R. L. Stevenson wrote the novel, he couldn't have known that his fictional pirate, Long John Silver, would become the world's classic high-seas rogue. For Silver is indeed a legend: No real pirate has been known to have a parrot, a peg leg, *and* a treasure map. Maybe he lost his eyepatch?

The Right Light

Coming from a family of lighthouse engineers gave Stevenson inside knowledge about ships and navigation.

Breath of Fresh Blood

Stevenson was often sick. When he started coughing up blood, he decided to give his hemorrhaging lung a pirate name— "Bloody Jack."

"Fifteen men on the dead man's chest

Yo ho ho and a bottle of rum!"

Stevenson's pirates chant these lines to strike terror into the hearts of readers. They've since been made famous in a song from a 1901 Broadway musical based on *Treasure Island*.

R.L.Stevenson

Robert Louis Stevenson was born in Scotland in 1850. His father wanted him to become a civil engineer, but he dreamed of a writing career. Sick in bed in 1873, Stevenson wrote his first published essay and began to create a name for himself. After marrying Fanny Osborne in 1880, he spent the rest of his life writing and following the warm weather that helped his ailing lungs. He died in the Samoan Islands in 1894.

Selected Bibliography:

Treasure Island 1883
A Child's Garden of Verses 1885
Kidnapped 1886
The Strange Case of Dr. Jekyll and Mr. Hyde 1886
The Black Arrow 1888

Main characters	Jim Hawkins, the young narrator Billy Bones, a sailor with a dubious scar Dr. Livesey, the Hawkins' family friend	Long John Silver, "cook" on the *Hispaniola* Captain Flint, Silver's parrot Captain Flint, a dead, once deadly, pirate

When he meets Billy Bones, young Jim Hawkins has no idea that he'll soon embark on a dangerous adventure. But then the old sailor dies—and Jim ends up with his most prized possession: the treasure map of the notorious Captain Flint. Soon Jim secures a ship and sets off to find buried riches. He'll need big-time bravery, however, for the pirate Long John Silver has disguised himself as the ship's cook—and will stop at nothing to make the treasure his own!

Polly Want a Piece of Eight?

Silver named his parrot for the terrible pirate Flint, so it's no surprise that the bird's favorite squawk is a pirate's favorite loot: "Pieces of eight! Pieces of eight!"

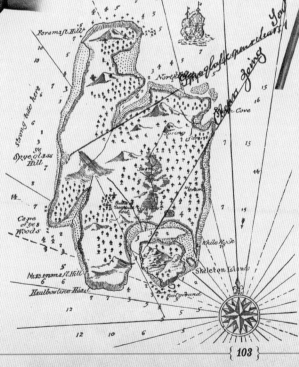

Fearsome Friend

Long John Silver was modeled after Stevenson's friend William Henley, a fellow writer who used a crutch and had thick curly hair and a beard.

Mapping It Out

When his stepson drew an imaginary "treasure island," Stevenson dreamt up a pirate captain whose map launches a young boy's adventure. He wrote a chapter a day and read the story out loud to his family in the evenings.

ON SKELETON ISLAND, Jim Hawkins has fallen into the hands of Long John Silver and his pirate crew. According to the treacherous Captain Flint's map, the treasure should be close by. But as the pirates begin to decode Flint's mysterious message, they discover more than they bargained for…

We made a curious figure, had anyone been there to see us; all in soiled sailor clothes, and all but me armed to the teeth. Silver had two guns slung about him—one before and one behind—besides the great cutlass at his waist, and a pistol in each pocket of his square-tailed coat. To complete his strange appearance, Captain Flint sat perched upon his shoulder and gabbling odds and ends of purposeless sea talk. I had a line about my waist, and followed obediently after the sea cook, who held the loose end of the rope, now in his free hand, now between his powerful teeth. For all the world, I was led like a dancing bear.

The other men were variously burdened; some carrying picks and shovels—for that had been the very first necessary they brought ashore from the *Hispaniola*—others laden with pork, bread, and brandy for the midday meal…. Well, thus equipped, we all set out—even the fellow with the broken head, who should certainly have kept in shadow—and straggled, one after another, to the beach, where the two gigs awaited us. Even these bore trace of the drunken folly of the pirates, one in a broken thwart, and both in their muddied and unbaled condition. Both were to be carried along with us, for the sake of safety; and so, with our numbers divided between them, we set forth upon the bosom of the anchorage.

As we pulled over, there was some discussion on the chart. The red cross was, of course, far too large to be a guide; and the terms of the note on the back, as you will hear, admitted of some ambiguity. They ran, the reader may remember, thus:

"Tall tree, Spy-glass Shoulder, bearing a point to the N. of N.N.E. Skeleton Island E.S.E. and by E. Ten feet."

A tall tree was thus the principal mark. Now, right before us, the anchorage was bounded by a plateau from two to three hundred feet high, adjoining on the north the sloping southern shoulder of the Spy-glass, and rising again towards the south into the rough cliffy eminence called the Mizzenmast Hill. The top of the plateau was dotted thickly with pine trees of varying height. Every here and there, one of a different species rose forty or fifty feet clear above its neighbors, and which of these was the particular "tall tree" of Captain Flint could only be decided on the spot, and by the readings of the compass.

Yet, although that was the case, every man on board the boats had picked a favorite of his own ere we were halfway over, Long John alone shrugging his shoulders and bidding them wait till they were there.

We pulled easily, by Silver's directions, not to weary the hands prematurely; and, after quite a long passage, landed at the mouth of the second river—that which runs down a woody cleft of the Spy-glass. Thence, bending to our left, we began to ascend the slope towards the plateau.

At the first outset, heavy, miry ground and a matter, marish vegetation, greatly delayed our progress; but by little and little the hill began to steepen and become stony under foot, and the wood to change its character and to grow in a more open order. It was, indeed, a most pleasant portion of the island that we were now approaching. A heavy-scented broom and many flowering shrubs had almost taken the place of grass. Thickets of green nutmeg trees were dotted here and there with the red columns and the broad shadow of the pines; and the first mingled their spice with the aroma of the others. The air, besides, was fresh and stirring, and this, under the sheer sunbeams, was a wonderful refreshment to our senses.

The party spread itself abroad, in a fan shape, shouting and leaping to and fro. About the center, and a good way behind the rest, Silver and I followed—I tethered by my rope, he ploughing, with deep pants, among the sliding gravel. From time to time, indeed, I had to lend him a hand, or he must have missed his footing and fallen backward down the hill.

We had thus proceeded for about half a mile, and were approaching the brow of the plateau, when the man upon the farthest left began to cry aloud, as if in terror. Shout after shout came from him, and the others began to run in his direction.

"He can't 'a found the treasure," said old Morgan, hurrying past us from the right, "for that's clean a-top." Indeed, as we found when we also reached the spot, it was something very different. At the foot of a pretty big pine, and involved in a green creeper, which had even partly lifted some of the smaller bones, a human skeleton lay, with a few shreds of clothing, on the ground. I believe a chill struck for a moment to every heart.

"He was a seaman," said George Merry, who, bolder than the rest, had gone up close, and was examining the rags of clothing. "Leastways, this is good sea cloth."

"Ay, ay," said Silver, "like enough; you wouldn't look to find a bishop here, I reckon. But what sort of a way is that for bones to lie? 'Tain't in natur'."

Indeed, on a second glance, it seemed impossible to fancy that the body was in a natural position. But for some disarray (the work, perhaps, of the birds that had fed upon him, or of the growing creeper that had gradually enveloped his remains) the man lay perfectly straight—his feet pointing in one direction, his hands, raised above his head like a diver's, pointing directly in the opposite.

"I've taken a notion into my old numbskull," observed Silver. "Here's the compass; there's the tiptop of p'int o' Skeleton Island, stickin' out like a tooth. Just take a bearing, will you, along the line of them bones."

It was done. The body pointed straight in the direction of the island, and the compass read duly E. S. E. and by E.

"I thought so," cried the cook; "this here is a p'inter. Right up there is our line for the Pole Star and the jolly dollars. But, by thunder! If it don't make me cold inside to think of Flint. This is one of his jokes, and no mistake. Him and these six was alone here, he killed 'em, every man; and this one he hauled here and laid down by compass, shiver my timbers! They're long bones, and the hair's been yellow. Ay, that would be Allardyce. You mind Allardyce, Tom Morgan?"

"Ay, ay," returned Morgan. "I mind him; he owed me money, he did, and took my knife ashore with him."

"Speaking of knives," said another, "why don't we find his'n lying round? Flint warn't the man to pick a seaman's pocket, and the birds, I guess, would leave it be."

"By the powers, and that's true!" cried Silver.

"There ain't a thing left here," said

Merry, still feeling round among the bones, "not a copper dolt nor a baccy box. It don't look nat'ral to me."

"No, by gum, it don't," agreed Silver; "not nat'ral, nor not nice, says you. Great guns! messmates, but if Flint was living, this would be a hot spot for you and me. Six they were, and six are we; and bones is what they are now."

"I saw him dead with these here deadlights," said Morgan. "Billy took me in. There he laid, with penny pieces on his eyes."

"Dead—ay, sure enough he's dead and gone below," said the fellow with the bandage; "but if ever sperrit walked, it would be Flint's. Dear heart, but he died bad, did Flint!"

"Ay, that he did," observed another; "now he raged, and now he hollered for the rum, and now he sang. 'Fifteen Men' were his only song, mates; and I tell you true, I never rightly liked to hear it since. It was main hot, and the windy was open, and I hear that old song comin' out as clear as clear—and the death-haul on the man a'ready."

"Come, come," said Silver, "stow this talk. He's dead, and he don't walk, that I know; leastways, he won't walk by day, and you may lay to that. Care killed a cat. Fetch ahead for the doubloons."

We started, certainly; but in spite of the hot sun and the staring daylight, the pirates no longer ran separate and shouting through the wood, but kept side by side and spoke with bated breath. The terror of the dead buccaneer had fallen on their spirits.

(The men sat down for a rest.)

Silver, as he sat, took certain bearings with his compass. "There are three 'tall trees,'" said he, "about in the right line from Skeleton Island. 'Spy-glass Shoulder,' I take it, means that lower p'int there. It's child's play to find the stuff now. I've half a mind to dine first."

"I don't feel sharp," growled Morgan. "Thinkin' o' Flint—I think it were—as done me."

"Ah, well, my son, you praise your stars he's dead," said Silver. . . .

Ever since they had found the skeleton and got upon this train of thought, they had spoken lower and lower, and they had almost got to whispering by now, so that the sound of their talk hardly interrupted the silence of the wood. All of a sudden, out of the middle of the trees in front of us, a thin, high, trembling voice struck up the well-known air and words:

"Fifteen men on the dead man's chest—
Yo-ho-ho, and a bottle of rum!"

Pirates of Penzance

In 1879, *The Pirates of Penzance* premiered in New York. At the time, American copyright laws did not protect foreign artists, so the Englishmen Gilbert and Sullivan chose to debut their new production in the U.S. to keep American opera companies from stealing it—as had happened with a previous show.

Pirate Joke

Gilbert and Sullivan poked fun at opera-stealing Americans with this title. Real-life Penzance was a peaceful place pirates would never think to plunder.

Musical Knights

Both Gilbert and Sullivan were knighted by the English crown: Sullivan by Queen Victoria in 1883, and Gilbert by King Edward VII in 1907.

Shiver Me Spinach

The theme for "Popeye the Sailor Man" was borrowed from the *Penzance* song "I Am the Pirate King."

Gilbert & Sullivan

Both English, **William Gilbert** and **Arthur Sullivan** were born in 1836 and 1842, respectively. During a 26-year partnership that began in 1870, the duo's most popular collaborations were comic operas. Gilbert wrote all the lyrics and dialogue, while Sullivan composed the music. Both men died of heart failure—Sullivan in 1900 and Gilbert in 1911 (while trying to rescue a young lady from his private lake).

Selected Bibliography:

Trial by Jury 1875
HMS Pinafore 1878
The Pirates of Penzance 1879
Iolanthe 1883
The Mikado 1885
Ruddigore 1887

Frederic was mistakenly apprenticed to pirates when his childhood nurse misheard his father, who wished him to be a pilot. On his 21st birthday, Frederic can finally leave the cutthroats—who aren't very good pirates, anyway—and pursue a nobler fate. It's this very sense of duty, however, that gets him in trouble again and again, from when

he first meets Mabel and learns there exist women besides his old nurse (now fiancée!), to the hilarious final mix-up with his precise birth date.

King Kline

Kevin Kline starred as the Pirate King in this 1983 film adaptation of *Penzance*, as well as in a stage production at New York's Central Park.

The Pirate Movie

This 1982 spoof of *Penzance*, starring Christopher Atkins, is perhaps even sillier than the original.

Urban Pirates

Penzance played again in New York City, at the Symphony Space theater, in 1994.

ACT I. SCENE. A rocky seashore on the coast of Cornwall. In the distance is a calm sea, on which a schooner is lying at anchor. Rock L. sloping down to L.C. of stage. Under these rocks is a cavern, the entrance to which is seen at first entrance L. A natural arch of rock occupies the R.C. of the stage. As the curtain rises groups of pirates are discovered —some drinking, some playing cards. SAMUEL, the Pirate Lieutenant, is going from one group to another, filling the cups from a flask. FREDERIC is seated in a despondent attitude at the back of the scene. RUTH kneels at his feet.

Song No. 1—Act I

OPENING CHORUS:
ALL:
Pour, O pour the pirate sherry;
Fill, O fill the pirate glass;
And, to make us more than merry
Let the pirate bumper pass.

SAMUEL:
For today our pirate 'prentice
Rises from indentures freed;
Strong his arm, and keen his scent is
He's a pirate now indeed!

ALL:
Here's good luck to Fred'ric's ventures!
Fred'ric's out of his indentures.

SAMUEL:
Two and twenty, now he's rising,
And alone he's fit to fly,
Which we're bent on signalizing
With unusual revelry.

ALL:
Here's good luck to Fred'ric's ventures!
Fred'ric's out of his indentures.
Pour, O pour the pirate sherry;
Fill, O fill the pirate glass;
And, to make us more than merry
Let the pirate bumper pass.

Dialogue Following Song No. 1—Act I
(FREDERIC rises and comes forward with PIRATE KING, who enters)

KING:
Yes, Frederic, from to-day you rank as a full-blown member of our band.

ALL:
Hurrah!

FREDERIC:
My friends, I thank you all, from my heart, for your kindly wishes.
Would that I could repay them as they deserve!

KING:
What do you mean?

FREDERIC:
To-day I am out of my indentures, and to-day I leave you for ever.

KING:
But this is quite unaccountable; a keener hand at scuttling a Cunarder or cutting out a White Star never shipped a handspike.

FREDERIC:
Yes, I have done my best for you. And why? It was my duty under my indentures, and I am the slave of duty. As a child I was regularly apprenticed to your band. It was through an error—no matter, the mistake was ours, not yours, and I was in honour bound by it.

SAMUEL:
An error? What error? (RUTH rises and comes forward)

FREDERIC:
I may not tell you; it would reflect upon my well-loved Ruth.

RUTH:
Nay, dear master, my mind has long been gnawed by the cankering tooth of mystery. Better have it out at once.

Song No. 2 — Act I

RUTH:
When Frederic was a little lad
he proved so brave and daring,
His father thought he'd 'prentice
him to some career seafaring.
I was, alas! his nurs'rymaid,
and so it fell to my lot
To take and bind the promising
boy apprentice to a pilot—
A life not bad for a hardy lad,
though surely not a high lot,
Though I'm a nurse, you might
do worse than make your boy a pilot.

I was a stupid nurs'rymaid,
on breakers always steering,
And I did not catch the word aright,
through being hard of hearing;
Mistaking my instructions,
which within my brain did gyrate,
I took and bound this promising boy
apprentice to a pirate.
A sad mistake it was to make
and doom him to a vile lot.
I bound him to a pirate—you!
—instead of to a pilot.

Dialogue Following Song No. 2 — Act I

RUTH:
Oh, pardon! Frederic, pardon! (Kneels)

FREDERIC:
Rise, sweet one, I have long pardoned you. (Ruth rises)

RUTH:
The two words were so much alike!

FREDERIC:
They were. They still are, though years have rolled over their heads. But this afternoon my obligation ceases. Individually, I love you all with affection unspeakable; but, collectively, I look upon you with a disgust that amounts to absolute detestation. Oh! pity me, my beloved friends, for such is my sense of duty that, once out of my indentures, I shall feel myself bound to devote myself heart and soul to your extermination!

ALL:
Poor lad—poor lad! (All weep)

KING:
Well, Frederic, if you conscientiously feel that it is your duty to destroy us, we cannot blame you for acting on that conviction. Always act in accordance with the dictates of your conscience, my boy, and chance the consequences.

SAMUEL:
Besides, we can offer you but little temptation to remain with us. We don't seem to make piracy pay. I'm sure I don't know why, but we don't.

FREDERIC:
I know why, but, alas! I mustn't tell you; it wouldn't be right.

KING:
Why not, my boy? It's only half-past eleven, and you are one of us until the clock strikes twelve.

SAMUEL:
True, and until then you are bound to protect our interests.

ALL:
Hear, hear!

FREDERIC:
Well, then, it is my duty, as a pirate, to tell you that you are too tender-hearted. For instance, you make a point of never attacking a weaker party than yourselves, and when you attack a stronger party you invariably get thrashed.

KING:
There is some truth in that.

FREDERIC:
Then, again, you make a point of never molesting an orphan!

SAMUEL:
Of course: we are orphans ourselves, and know what it is.

FREDERIC:
Yes, but it has got about, and what is the consequence? Every one we capture says he's an orphan. The last three ships we took proved to be manned entirely by orphans, and so we had to let them go. One would think that Great Britain's mercantile navy was recruited solely from her orphan asylums—which we know is not the case.

SAMUEL:
But, hang it all! you wouldn't have us absolutely merciless?

FREDERIC:
There's my difficulty; until twelve o'clock I would, after twelve I wouldn't. Was ever a man placed in so delicate a situation?

RUTH:
And Ruth, your own Ruth, whom you love so well, and who has won her middle-aged way into your boyish heart, what is to become of her?

KING:
Oh, he will take you with him.

FREDERIC:
Well, Ruth, I feel some difficulty about you. It is true that I admire you very much, but I have been constantly at sea since I was eight years old, and yours is the only woman's face I have seen during that time. I think it is a sweet face.

RUTH:
It is—oh, it is!

FREDERIC:
I say I think it is; that is my impression. But as I have never had an opportunity of comparing you with other women, it is just possible I may be mistaken.

(To discover Ruth's fate, see the play! For the scene's end, read on. . .)

KING:
Well, it's the top of the tide, and we must be off. Farewell, Frederic. When your process of extermination begins, let our deaths be as swift and painless as you can conveniently make them.

FREDERIC:
I will! By the love I have for you, I swear it! Would that you could render this extermination unnecessary by accompanying me back to civilization!

KING:
No, Frederic, it cannot be. I don't think much of our profession, but, contrasted with respectability, it is comparatively honest. No, Frederic, I shall live and die a Pirate King.

Peter Pan

Peter Pan first appeared in J. M. Barrie's "The Little White Bird," the tale of a bird who becomes a child, only to find himself stuck in a stroller. When he learns to fly again, he soars all the way to Neverland and meets Peter Pan—a minor character whose major popularity inspired Barrie to write Peter a starring role. The play, "Peter and Wendy," was later turned into the book *Peter Pan*.

Friendly Suggestion

A young girl who couldn't pronounce her *r*'s called Barrie "my friendy"—it sounded like "Wendy," and soon Barrie had a name for Peter's best friend.

Peter Pan was inspired by Barrie's dear friends, the Llewelyn-Davies brothers. The author became the boys' legal guardian after their parents died of cancer.

The Llewelyn-Davies family

James Matthew Barrie was born in Scotland in 1860. When his older brother David died tragically at age 14, James spent the rest of his childhood trying to replace his mother's most beloved son. He made such efforts that when he reached 14, he stopped growing. The five-foot-tall man married actress Mary Ansell in 1894, but never had any children, choosing instead to celebrate his many young friends and their endless imaginations in stories. Barrie died in 1937.

J. M. Barrie

Selected Bibliography:

Auld Licht Idylls 1888
Ibsen's Ghost 1891
The Little White Bird 1901
The Admirable Crichton 1902
Peter and Wendy, renamed *Peter Pan* 1911
The Boy David 1936

Main characters	**Peter Pan**, the boy who will never grow up **Tinkerbell**, a fairy whose dust helps kids fly **The Lost Boys**, orphans who live in Neverland	**Wendy Darling**, "mother" to the Lost Boys **Michael and John Darling**, Wendy's brothers **Captain Hook**, the villainous pirate

Peter Pan and the Lost Boys live on an island called Neverland, where they never have to grow up. They take care of themselves—and that's how they like it—but sometimes they miss their mothers' stories. So Peter often flies to the Darling nursery to hear Mrs. Darling's tales, which he then brings back to Neverland. On one such visit, Peter meets Wendy and decides she would make a great mother for the Lost Boys. But Wendy won't leave her younger brothers behind, and thus begins a wild adventure— which includes a run-in with the notorious pirate, Captain Hook!

1904 Stage Debut

After Nina Boucicault, who played Peter, said "Clap your hands if you believe in fairies," she was so relieved at the audience's enthusiasm that she burst into tears of joy.

Not the Devil's Work

Barrie wanted this statue of Peter in London's Kensington Gardens to be modeled after Michael Llewelyn-Davies. The artist refused, and when Barrie saw the finished work, he noted, "It doesn't show the devil in Peter!"

Finding Neverland

This heart-wrenching 2004 film tells the story of Barrie and the Llewelyn-Davies family, including the fun they had in their elaborate games— like playing pirates!

Captain Sharkey

Most famous for his Sherlock Holmes stories, Arthur Conan Doyle also wrote of the abominable Captain Sharkey. This frightening pirate's exploits were first introduced in 1900, in a story collection called *The Green Flag*, and were followed by further tales of treachery in 1922's *The Dealings of Captain Sharkey and Other Tales of Pirates*.

Spirit Crystal

Doyle embraced spiritualism, and believed there was scientific proof of an afterlife.

The Coming of the Fairies

Although many smelled a hoax, Doyle wrote an entire book defending the honesty of two girls from Cottingley, England, whose photographs allegedly showed them with fairies.

Sorry, Sherlock

In Sherlock Holmes, Doyle created one of literature's first logic-driven crime solvers. Hoping to devote time to his other interests (like swashbucklers and spirits), Doyle killed Holmes in 1893—but was forced to bring him back by popular demand.

Sir Arthur Conan Doyle was born in England in 1859. After serving as a doctor in the South African Boer War, he wrote a pamphlet justifying Britain's role, for which he was knighted in 1902. Later, as an eye doctor, he had a lot of time to write, for "not a single patient crossed [his] door." Doyle was married twice, had a total of five children, and produced far more stories than centipedes have legs. He died from a heart attack in 1930.

Arhutr Conan Doyle

Selected Bibliography:

The Adventures of Sherlock Holmes 1892

The Great Boer War 1900

The Hound of the Baskervilles 1902

The Lost World 1912

Coming of the Fairies 1922

The Dealings of Captain Sharkey and Other Pirate Tales 1922

Main characters	**Captain John Sharkey**, a wicked pirate	**Sir Charles Ewan**, the governor of St. Kitt's
	Ned Galloway, Sharkey's quartermaster	**Stephen Craddock**, who tries to catch Sharkey
	Captain Scarrow, a stout sailor with bad luck	**Copley Banks**, a merchant turned pirate

The first three tales of Sharkey are tragic for his victims, whose reputations, families, and often very lives are lost in their encounters. Captain Scarrow, upon whose ship Sharkey appears dressed as a governor; Stephen Craddock, who tries to trap the pirate during his ritual careening; and Copley Banks, a respectable man who turns pirate to extract revenge, are three such unfortunate fellows. In fact, Sharkey is such an unstoppable villain that when he seems to be shark bait at last, he reappears where least expected—and least welcome.

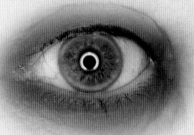

Gruesome Glance

Captain Sharkey's eerie eyes struck terror in the hearts of any unfortunate enough to meet him, for they were "of the lightest filmy blue with red-rimmed lids."

Deadly Deliverance

Captain Sharkey prowled the Caribbean Sea in the *Happy Delivery*. Also known as the "barque of death," this coal-black ship made seamen both honest and dishonest tremble when they spotted its sinister shape on the horizon.

UPON LEAVING ST. KITT'S, Scarrow's ship contains two unusual guests: an American, whose ship was scuttled by Sharkey, and the island's governor, Sir Charles, who recently ordered the jailed pirate hanged. Unfortunately, it turns out there's more to these passengers than meets the eye...

The boatswain had the watch, and the three friends were met for a last turn of cards in the cabin, the faithful American still serving as eyes to the Governor. There was a good stake upon the table, for the sailors had tried on this last night to win their losses back from their passenger. Suddenly he threw his cards down, and swept all the money into the pocket of his long-flapped silken waistcoat.

"The game's mine!" said he.

"Heh, Sir Charles, not so fast!" cried Captain Scarrow; "you have not played out the hand, and we are not the losers."

"Sink you for a liar!" said the Governor. "I tell you I have played out the hand, and that you are a loser." He whipped off his wig and his glasses as he spoke, and there was a high, bald forehead, and a pair of shifty blue eyes with the red rims of a bull terrier.

"Good God!" cried the mate.

"It's Sharkey!"

The two sailors sprang from their seats, but the big American castaway had put his huge back against the cabin door, and he held a pistol in each of his hands. The passenger had also laid a pistol upon the scattered cards in front of him, and he burst into his high, neighing laugh.

"Captain Sharkey is the name, gentlemen," said he, "and this is Roaring Ned Galloway, the quartermaster of the *Happy Delivery*. We made it hot, and so they marooned us: me on a dry Tortuga cay, and him in an oarless boat. You dogs—you poor, fond, water-hearted dogs—we hold you at the end of our pistols!"

"You may shoot, or you may not!" cried Scarrow, striking his hand upon the breast of his frieze jacket. "If it's my last breath, Sharkey, I tell you that you are a bloody rogue and miscreant, with a halter and hell-fire in store for you!"

"There's a man of spirit, and one of my own kidney, and he's going to make a very pretty death of it!" cried Sharkey. "There's no one aft save the man at the wheel, so you may keep your breath, for you'll need it soon. Is the dinghy astern, Ned?"

"Ay, ay, captain!"

"And the other boats scuttled?"

"I bored them all in three places."

"Then we shall have to leave you, Captain Scarrow. You look as if you hadn't quite got your bearings yet. Is there anything you'd like to ask me?"

"I believe you're the devil himself!" cried the captain. "Where is the Governor of St. Kitt's?"

"When last I saw him his Excellency was in bed with his throat cut. When I broke prison I learnt from my friends— for Captain Sharkey has those who love him in every port—that the Governor was starting for Europe under a master who had never seen him. I climbed his verandah, and I paid him the little debt that I owed him. Then I came aboard you with such of his things as I had need of, and a pair of glasses to hide these tell-tale eyes of mine, and I have ruffled it as a governor should. Now, Ned, you can get to work upon them."

"Help! help! Watch ahoy!" yelled the mate; but the butt of the pirate's pistol crashed down on his head, and he dropped like a pithed ox. Scarrow rushed for the door, but the sentinel clapped his hand over his mouth, and threw his other arm round his waist.

"No use, Master Scarrow," said Sharkey. "Let us see you go down on your knees and beg for your life."

"I'll see you—" cried Scarrow, shaking his mouth clear.

"Twist his arm round, Ned. Now will you?"

"No; not if you twist it off."

"Put an inch of your knife into him."

"You may put six inches, and then I won't."

"Sink me, but I like his spirit!" cried Sharkey. "Put your knife in your pocket, Ned. You've saved your skin, Scarrow, and it's a pity so stout a man should not take to the only trade where a pretty fellow can pick up a living. You must be born for no common death, Scarrow, since you have lain at my mercy and lived to tell the story. Tie him up, Ned."

"To the stove, captain?"

"Tut, tut! there's a fire in the stove. None of your rover tricks, Ned Galloway, unless they are called for, or I'll let you know which of us two is captain and which is quartermaster. Make him fast to the table."

"Nay, I thought you meant to roast him!" said the quartermaster.

STEPHEN CRADDOCK plans to capture Sharkey by luring him onto the *White Rose*, a replica of the *Happy Delivery*. In this scene, Craddock returns to the *Rose* after searching an island for the pirate captain—only to discover that he's not the only one able to perpetrate nautical switcheroos!

"What roguery is this?" shouted Craddock, looking furiously around him.

But the crew stood in knots about the deck, laughing and whispering . . . . Craddock noticed that they were dressed in the most singular manner, with long riding-coats, full-skirted velvet gowns and coloured ribands at their knees, more like men of fashion than seamen.

As he looked at their grotesque figures he struck his brow with his clenched fist to be sure that he was awake. The deck seemed to be much dirtier than when he had left it, and there were strange, sun-blackened faces turned upon him from every side. Not one of them did he know save only Joshua Hird. Had the ship been captured in his absence? Were these Sharkey's men who were around him? At the thought he broke furiously away and tried to climb over to his boat, but a dozen hands were on him in an instant, and he was pushed aft through the open door of his own cabin.

And it was all different to the cabin which he had left. The floor was different, the ceiling was different, the furniture was different. His had been plain and austere. This was sumptuous and yet dirty, hung with rare velvet curtains splashed with wine-stains, and panelled with costly woods which were pocked with pistol-marks.

On the table was a great chart of the Caribbean Sea, and beside it, with compasses in his hand, sat a clean-shaven, pale-faced man with a fur cap and a claret-colored coat of damask. Craddock turned white under his freckles as he looked upon the long, thin high-nostrilled nose and the red-rimmed eyes which were turned upon him with the fixed, humorous gaze of the master player who has left his opponent without a move.

"Sharkey!" cried Craddock.

Sharkey's thin lips opened, and he broke into his high, sniggering laugh.

"You fool!" he cried, and, leaning over, he stabbed Craddock's shoulder again and again with his compasses. "You poor, dull-witted fool, would you match yourself against me?"

UPSTANDING SUGAR MERCHANT Copley Banks turned pirate, spent two years on the seas, and befriended Sharkey. Still, Sharkey always refused to board Banks's ship, but finally agrees to visit Copley (and his dumb sevant) after one really good raid…

"Captain Sharkey," said Copley Banks, "do you remember the Duchess of Cornwall, hailing from London, which you took and sank three years ago off the Statira Shoal?"

"Curse me if I can bear their names in mind," said Sharkey. "We did as many as ten ships a week about that time."

"There were a mother and two sons among the passengers. Maybe that will bring it back to your mind."

Captain Sharkey leant back in thought, with his huge thin beak of a nose jutting upwards. Then he burst suddenly into a high treble, neighing laugh. He remembered it, he said, and he added details to prove it.

"But burn me if it had not slipped from my mind!" he cried. "How came you to think of it?"

"It was of interest to me," said Copley Banks, "for the woman was my wife, and the lads were my only sons."

Sharkey stared across at his companion, and saw that the smouldering fire which lurked always in his eyes had burned up into a lurid flame. He read their menace, and he clapped his hands to his empty belt. Then he turned to seize a weapon, but the bight of a rope was cast round him, and in an instant his arms were bound to his side. He fought like a wild cat, and screamed for help. "Ned!" he yelled. "Ned! Wake up! Here's damned villainy! Help, Ned!—help!"

But the three men were far too deeply sunk in their swinish sleep for any voice to wake them. Round and round went the rope, until Sharkey was swathed like a mummy from ankle to neck. The dumb man chattered in his exultation, and Sharkey winced for the first time when he saw the empty mouth before him. He understood that vengeance, slow and patient, had dogged him long, and clutched him at last…

…Wriggle as he would he could not move an inch either to the right or left…so that there was no chance that he should work free.

"Now, you bloody devil," said Copley Banks, softly, "you must listen to what I have to say to you, for they are the last words that you will hear. …"

Just a Few More!

Although the Golden Age of Piracy is long gone, writers have been creating new nautical adventures ever since. Here are some of the most popular and influential, but there are many more to be discovered—think of all the swashbuckling journeys you have yet to undertake!

Most Myths Start Here

Captain Charles Johnson—possibly an alias for Daniel Defoe—wrote *A General History of the Robberies and Murders of the Most Notorious Pyrates* in 1724. Although its tales are embellished with fiction, they have provided many of the most enduring legends about Blackbeard, Anne Bonny, and other famous pirates.

First Steps

There is only one real-life case, but most people think walking the plank was incredibly common—thanks to the 1837 work: *The Pirates' Own Book: Authentic Narratives of the Most Celebrated Sea Robbers*.

Daniel Defoe (1660–1731)

This English author wrote of seafaring adventure in both *Robinson Crusoe* and *Captain Singleton*, the story of a kidnapped boy who grows up to be a ruthless pirate. Defoe himself was no stranger to daring exploits—he had a day job as a government spy!

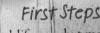

The Pirates' Own Book by Charles Ell...

The Tryal of Captain Kidd by Don Seitz

FANNY CAMPBELL,
THE FEMALE PIRATE CAPTAIN.

Portrait of the Female Pirate.

BY LIEUTENANT MURRAY.

BOSTON:
PUBLISHED BY F. GLEASON, 1 1-2 TREMONT ROW.
1845.

Gripping Courtroom Drama

Based on actual courtroom transcripts, as well as on letters from Captain Kidd and his original financial backers, Don Seitz's *The Tryal Of Captain William Kidd* showcases 17th century piracy and the inner workings of British politics. It was published in 1935.

Rising in the Ranks

An action-packed sea story, *Fanny Campbell* first appeared in 1845. The author, 25-year-old Maturin Ballou—who wrote as "Lieutenant Murray"—must have been thrilled: *Fanny* sold 80,000 copies in just a few months!

Good and Evil

The Coral Island, R.M. Ballantyne's 1858 sea yarn about three boys who are stranded on an island, inspired William Golding to write *Lord of the Flies* in 1954. Golding uses the names of some of Ballantyne's characters, but changes the story. Instead of thriving on the island, the *Flies* boys form tribes and treat one another viciously.

Lord of the Flies by William Golding

Index

Further Pirate Resources

For a timber-shivering list of pirate Web links, as well as an ocean's worth of suggestions for further reading, please visit: http://www.kiddk.com/piratepedia

Acknowledgments

A hearty many deserve a barrel of delicious grog for their work on this project: Engly Chang and Lani Choi for design and repro work, Melissa Hom for her cartography talents, Katherine Yam and her team at Colourscan for color reproduction, and the fabulous pirate literature researcher. Alisha and Alan would also like to thank the office vending machine for its mind-blowing snacks, the creators of soda for their great contribution to creative spirit, and our awesome friends and family. Tai sends an "Arrr!" to Dino, Wumei, and Shirobe Blanche for all their love and support. Musket balls to all!

Photo credits

AKG Images – 28bl. Alamy: Alan King 52b; bigfishphotoagent 117tr; Jon Arnold Images 91tl; JupiterMedia 11t; Lebrecht Music and Arts Photo Library 10 bc; Leslie Garland Picture Library 90cl; Mary Evans Picture Library 11tr, 21b, 102-103tr, 22tr, 23cr, 24br, 26cl, 28tl, 29br, 32 b, 47tl, 48r, 54, 57tl, 59tl, 75tl, 75bl, 102-103bl, 123tl; North Wind Picture Archives 15b, 46tr, 75r, 98tr; Patrick Eden 117b; PhotoSpin, Inc 93tr; Pictorial Press Ltd 89cl, 97tl, 123bl; POPPERFOTO 26cr, 41bl; Purestock 78b; Robert Fried 23cl, 25b; Thinkstock 90l; Visual Arts Library (London) 122br. Art Resource, NY: HIP 14br; Erich Lessing 69r, 95br. AP WideWorld Photos: 88tl, 92c. Bridgeman Art Library International: Portrait of an unknown Roman warrior 14bl; Galley Slaves of the Barbary Corsairs, Peter Newark Historical Pictures/The Bridgeman Art Library International 22bl; P493 Malta: the Grand Harbour of Valletta/© Wallace Collection, London, UK 28b; Galley Slaves of the Barbary Corsairs, Peter Newark Historical Pictures 29bl; The embarkation of the Knights of the Holy Spirit for the crusades/Bibliotheque des Arts Decoratifs, Paris, France, Archives Charmet 29cl; View of St. Malo, Private Collection/Giraudon 33tr; Possibly a portrait of Giovanni Da Verrazzano/© Collection of the New-

York Historical Society, USA, 39br; A View of the Town of St. George on the Island of Grenada/Private Collection, 51bl; The City of Charleston/© Collection of the New-York Historical Society, USA, 61br; Mary Read, Private Collection, Archives Charmet 61cl; The Capture of the Pirate Blackbeard, Private Collection, 67bl; Marooned, 1909 (oil on canvas)/© Delaware Art Museum, Wilmington, USA, Museum Purchase 69b; West View of Newgate, c.1810, Guildhall Art Gallery, City of London, 73tl; So the Treasure was Divided/ © Delaware Art Museum, Wilmington, USA, Howard Pyle Collection 77b. Corbis: Asian Art & Archaeology, Inc. 86 bc; Bettman 102-103crs; 35bc, 44tl, 44b, 45tr, 59br, 60tl, 60tc, 60tr; Blue Lantern Studio 114tl; Bruce Adams; Eye Ubiquitous 67br; Charles & Josette Lenars 16b; Christie's Images 81cl; Corbis 52 tl, 83 tl, 123 tr; Darrell Gulin 36b; Historical Picture Archive 32 bc, 35 tl, 37 tc, 114 bc, 115 tr; Joel W. Rogers 41br; Joel W. Rogers 99cl; Keren Su 35tr; Kevin Schafer 92tl; Krause, Johansen/Archivo Iconografico, SA 34 tr, 40 t; Lake County Museum 89br, 94 cr; Lee Snider/Photo Images 109b; Reuters 34tc, 37 br, 90 b, 99 tl, 99 cr; Richard T. Nowitz 92bl; Stapleton Collection 89br; Underwood & Underwood 122cl. The Master and Fellows of Corpus Christi College, Cambridge: 20tcl. DK Images: 20tcr, 22tl, 29tl, 39l, 43t, 45bl, 45bl, 48tl, 54tl, 59tr, 62bl, 62cr, 64ct,

64cb, 78tr, 81cr, 84tcl, 115tl; Peter Anderson (c) Danish National Museum 19br, 19bl; Peter Anderson (c) Dorling Kindersley, Courtesy of the Statens Historiska Museum, Stockholm 19c; Courtesy of the Musee de Saint-Malo, France 33cl, 72b, 75tc; (c) The British Museum 12tr, 12cl, 13tl, 13tr,19r, 37cl, 38bl; Tina Chambers 13bl, 24bl, 32bl, 33cr, 45tl, 45br, 49cl, 50tl, 50tcl, 50tcr, 50tr, 51tc, 51br, 54cl, 54cr, 56bl, 56br, 57br, 61tc, 63tl, 63tr, 63br, 64, 65tr, 65cr, 67tl, 67tc, 68bl, 68br, 73tr, 95cr; Courtesy of the Rye Town Council, East Sussex 73c; Alan Keohane 97tr; Dave King 69clb, 77tl, 89tl; Dave King (c) Dorling Kindersley, Courtesy of the Pitt Rivers Museum, University of Oxford 86l; Peter Robinson (c) Museum of the Order of St John, London 28ct, 28cb, 28bl, 29tr; James Stevenson (c) Dorling Kindersley, Courtesy of the National Maritime Museum, London 43cl, 58tl, 58tr, 66br, 70c, 70tl, 76l, 76bc; Clive Streeter 15tl; Colin Keates (c) Dorling Kindersley, Courtesy of the Natural History Museum, London 12bl; Courtesy of Oxford University Museum of Natural History, Gary Ombler (c) Dorling Kindersley 12br; Wilberforce House (c) Hull Museums 57l; Michel Zabe 34bl, 37cl. Getty Images: 47bc, 64b, 66c, 67tr. Great Ormond Street Hospital: Photograph of Llewellyn Davies Family by JM Barrie, reproduced with kind permission of Great Ormond Street Hospital for

Children, London 114c. IMB Piracy Reporting Centre: 91cr. Istockphoto. com: 94tr, 102-103bl. Library of Congress: 108tl, 108cl, 116bc. Courtesy of the Musee de Saint-Malo, France: 33cl, 72b, 75tc. Mary Evans Picture Library: 13br, 27r. National Maritime Museum, London: 18b, 20tl, 22br, 25tr, 26b, 29br, 27bl, 29tl, 34tl, 35cl, 37bl, 38br, 39tr, 41tl, 42tl, 42b, 43tr, 43br, 46tl, 49tl, 49br, 53tl 55tcl, 55tr, 55b, 55br, 58b, 59bl, 62br, 65tl, 65br, 68cl, 69tl, 69cl, 69cr, 70c, 73br, 76tr, 77tr, 79tr, 79bc, 80tl, 81br, 81tl, 82cr, 82br, 82bl, 83bc, 83r, 84tl, 93br, 122tl. North Carolina Maritime Museum: 93tl. The Picture Desk: The Art Archive 57tr, 74t, 85b; 20TH CENTURY FOX/THE KOBAL COLLECTION 96c, 109cl; CAROLCO/THE KOBAL COLLECTION 96cr; FILM COLONY/THE KOBAL COLLECTION 115br; HOOK PRODS/AMBLIN/THE KOBAL COLLECTION 97br; PARAMOUNT/WALT DISNEY PRODUCTIONS/ THE KOBAL COLLECTION 108tr; UNIVERSAL/ THE KOBAL COLLECTION 109cr; WARNER BROS/FIRST NATIONAL/THE KOBAL COLLECTION 96bl. www. piratesinparadise.com: 94bl. Science & Society Picture Library: NMPFT/ Science & Society Picture Library 116cl; Zentralbibliothek Zürich: 20tr.